Hits Quiz

Paul Gambaccini
Tim Rice
Jonathan Rice

Editorial Associate:
Tony Brown

D0318533

GUINNESS PUBLISHING

Acknowledgements

The authors would like to thank Jan Rice, Eileen Heinink, Alex Rice and Stephen Banks for their help in getting this book together. Thanks go to London Features International for the photographs.

Editor: Honor Head
Assistant Editor: Paola Simoneschi
Design: Cathy Shilling
Picture Research: Julie O'Leary

First published 1990 in Great Britain by Guinness Publishing Ltd,
33 London Road, Enfield, Middlesex

Typeset by Ace Filmsetting Ltd, Frome, Somerset

Printed and bound in Great Britain by The Bath Press, Bath

'Guinness' is a registered trade mark of Guinness Superlatives Ltd

ISBN 0-85112-928-5

Introduction

The question is, why the questions? Well, anybody who listens to music on the BBC or independent radio stations will have discovered that the only thing that every programme and every DJ seems to find room for (apart from the music itself, and some presenters have very little of that) is a quiz. Popular music and the charts have created questions needing urgent answers ever since Lita Roza asked 'How Much Is That Doggie In The Window?' in 1953, and there is no relief in sight. It seems that people like being asked questions and even more, they like knowing the answers. Our books, *British Hit Singles*, *British Hit Albums* and *Hits of the 80s* to name but three, have been used for so long as the source of answers to all these questions, that we thought it was about time we asked a few of our own. So here they are, all 2602 of them.

If you want to cheat, arm yourselves with our other publications and you will be able to find out many of the answers. However, there will still be plenty of questions which no amount of reference books will help you with, and others you won't believe even when you look up the answers. Still, time spent answering these questions is quieter than time spent at the Who concert of 31 May 1976, at least until the arguments start, and they will probably take longer to work out than Band Aid II's entire chart career.

Have fun.

Paul Gambaccini
Tim Rice
Jonathan Rice

Scoring system

Most of the quizzes are divided into three sections, A, B and (you guessed it) C. We believe that the questions in the A sections are the easiest, the B section questions are a little harder, and the C section questions are the Daddy Bear questions, the hardest of all. If you want to score your answers, give yourself 1 point for each correct A question, 2 for every B question and 3 for every C question solved.

Some quizzes have different rules which are explained at the beginning of each quiz. Follow the instructions and award marks accordingly.

1 First Picture Of You

The titles listed below were the first British hits for well-established acts. Name the act.

A

1 'Waterloo'
2 'Anarchy In The UK'
3 'Four From Toyah'
4 'Making Your Mind Up'
5 'Tainted Love'
6 'West End Girls'
7 'Virginia Plain'
8 'No Woman No Cry'
9 'I Should Be So Lucky'
10 'Do You Really Want To Hurt Me'
11 'Relax'
12 'Young Guns (Go For It)'
13 'In The Air Tonight'
14 'Sultans Of Swing'
15 'Saving All My Love For You'
16 'Seven Seas Of Rhye'
17 'Daddy Cool'
18 'Heartbreak Hotel'
19 'Holiday'
20 'Space Oddity'
21 'Are "Friends" Electric'
22 'Pictures Of Matchstick Men'
23 'Can't Stand Losing You'
24 'Never Gonna Give You Up'
25 'Your Song'

B

1 'Surfin' USA'
2 '(Get A) Grip (On Yourself)'
3 'Solsbury Hill'
4 'Don't Pay The Ferryman'
5 'I Know What I Like In Your Wardrobe'
6 'Dreaming Of Me'
7 'Come On'
8 'White Riot'
9 'Love Me Do'
10 'Hungry Heart'
11 'Dance Stance'
12 'Black Magic Woman'

13 'Stop Your Sobbin''
14 'In The City'
15 'Hot Dog'
16 'Running Free'
17 'Reach Out And Touch'
18 'How Sweet It Is'
19 'The Prince'
20 'Fool (If You Think It's Over)'
21 'Fire'
22 'This Will Be'
23 'You're The One For Me – Daybreak – A.M.'
24 'Just Like Me'
25 'Holiday 80'

1 'What You Need'
2 'Hardest Part Of The Night'
3 'Sheep'
4 'Love Meeting Love'
5 'Who Needs Love Like That'
6 'A Pair Of Brown Eyes'
7 'Dead Pop Stars'
8 'Fairplay'
9 'Last Night At Danceland'
10 'Wasted'
11 'Feels Like The First Time'
12 'Rescue'
13 'Life In A Day'
14 'Ceremony'
15 'Evergreen'
16 'Mary Ann'
17 'God's Kitchen'
18 'Rock And Roll Damnation'
19 'A Forest'
20 'Strummin''
21 'Chasing For The Breeze'
22 'Small Town Creed'
23 'Every Kinda People'
24 'Red Frame White Light'
25 'Market Square Heroes'

2 Miss You Like Crazy

In this quiz, we are looking for the missing word to make up two different names or song titles. So, for example, if the question is *I Love (   ) Can't Hurry Love*, the missing word is YOU. If it were *Olivia Newton-(   ) Travolta*, the answer would be JOHN. But they are not all quite as easy as that.

A

All these are the titles of British hit singles:

1 This Ole (   ) Of Fun
2 It's My (   ) Fears Two
3 Happy (   ) Talk
4 Edge Of (   ) Knows I'm Miserable Now
5 I'd Rather (   ) Your Body
6 West End (   ) On Film
7 You'll Never Walk (   ) Again Or
8 Dreams Of (   ) Of The Revolution
9 Don't Be (   ) Summer
10 Down (   ) Pressure
11 Ghost (   ) Called Malice
12 One Day In Your (   ) In A Northern Town
13 Turning (   ) Boy
14 China In Your (   ) On Your Heart
15 Eye Of The (   ) Feet
16 Deep (   ) Is On
17 Life In (   ) Joe
18 Hotel (   ) Girls
19 Get It (   ) The Inside
20 Merry Xmas (   ) Wants To Rule The World

B

All these are the titles of British hit albums:

1 Sgt Pepper's Lonely Hearts Club (   ) On The Run
2 Deepest (   ) Rain
3 Money For (   ) Like The Sun
4 Love (   ) From The Big Chair
5 Make It (   ) Area
6 Popped In Souled (   ) Of The Blue
7 Shaved (   ) People Tapes
8 Steel (   ) Of Steel
9 Tug Of (   ) Of The Worlds
10 We Too Are (   ) Step Beyond
11 The Final (   ) The Crap
12 Abbey (   ) To Hell

13 Ancient (   ) Of Stone

14 Back In (   ) Celebration

15 Be Yourself (   ) I'm Yours

16 With The (   ) For Sale

17 Labour Of (   ) Over Gold

18 Rubber (   )Mining

19 W.O. (   ) A.S.P.

20 See Jungle! See Jungle! Go Join Your Gang Yeah City All Over! Go
    Ape (   ) Nights

C All these acts have had British hit singles or albums, or both:

1 Little (   ) Marx

2 Gary (   ) Band

3 Ruby (   ) Head

4 Full (   ) MDs

5 Jeff (   ) Fontana

6 Real (   ) Shante

7 Kissing The (   ) Floyd

8 Jimmy (   ) Richard

9 Frankie Goes To (   ) Beyond

10 George (   ) Bolton

11 Modern (   ) Heads

12 Jackie (   ) Pickett

13 Brenda (   ) Marvin

14 Freddie (   ) Browne

15 Tommy (   ) Brown

16 Johnston (   ) Johnson

17 Iggy (   ) Will Eat Itself

18 Stevie (   ) Stuff

19 Boy (   ) Harrison

20 Grace (   ) Marie

3 The Oldest Swinger In Town

Too much sex, drugs and rock 'n' roll can take its toll on a pop star; others who have sworn by Oil Of Ulay for years have managed to slow down the ageing process. So who really are the Dinosaurs Of Rock?

A

Who is the oldest?

1 Smokey Robinson, Tom Robinson or Tom Petty
2 Michael Jackson, Joe Jackson or Joe Cocker
3 Billy Joel, Billy Ocean or Billy Idol
4 Robin, Barry or Maurice Gibb
5 Bobby Brown, Glenn Medeiros or Jason Donovan
6 Wilson Pickett, Johnny Mathis or Gene Chandler
7 Sandie Shaw, Petula Clark or Aretha Franklin
8 Paul Hardcastle, Howard Jones or Herbie Hancock
9 Paul McCartney, George Harrison or Ringo Starr
10 Ian Gillan, Robert Plant or Ozzy Osbourne
11 Bob Dylan, Leonard Cohen or Donovan
12 Bob Geldof, Midge Ure or Lionel Richie
13 Michael Jackson, Jermaine Jackson or Janet Jackson
14 Merrill Osmond, Donny Osmond or Little Jimmy Osmond
15 Rod Stewart, Jermaine Stewart or Andy Stewart
16 Frank Sinatra, Charles Aznavour or Max Bygraves
17 Eartha Kitt, Shirley Bassey or Nana Mouskouri
18 Jan Hammer, Vangelis or Mike Oldfield
19 Barry White, Teddy Pendergrass or Luther Vandross
20 Van Morrison, Eric Clapton or George Harrison
21 Rita Coolidge, Tammy Wynette or Linda Ronstadt
22 Annie Lennox, Pat Benatar or Olivia Newton-John
23 Jon Anderson, John Denver or Placido Domingo
24 Vic Damone, Perry Como or Herb Alpert
25 Martika, Toyah or Dana

B

Again, who is the oldest?

1 Bryan Adams, Morrissey or Thomas Dolby
2 Holly Johnson, Bono or Nick Heyward
3 Sade, Sheena Easton or Kim Wilde
4 Donny Osmond, Billy Bragg or Fish
5 Kate Bush, Madonna or Anita Baker
6 George Michael, Richard Marx or Terence Trent D'Arby
7 Sonia, Debbie Gibson or Tiffany
8 Natalie Cole, Joan Armatrading or Suzi Quatro

9   Chaka Khan, Randy Crawford or Grace Jones
10 Phil Collins, Chris Rea or David Cassidy
11 Peter Gabriel, Stevie Wonder or Bruce Springsteen
12 Alexander O'Neal, Adam Ant or Elvis Costello
13 Shakin' Stevens, Steve Winwood or Chris De Burgh
14 Alice Cooper, Meat Loaf or Sammy Hagar
15 Liza Minnelli, Bette Midler or Deborah Harry
16 David Bowie, Bryan Ferry or Al Green
17 Ray Charles, James Brown or Des O'Connor
18 Ella Fitzgerald, Vera Lynn or Doris Day
19 Dusty Springfield, Roberta Flack or Dionne Warwick
20 Cliff Richard, Tom Jones or Gary Glitter
21 Bill Wyman, Bill Withers or Ben E. King
22 Mick Jagger, Julio Iglesias or George Benson
23 Barbra Streisand, Diana Ross or Cilla Black
24 Malcolm McLaren, Iggy Pop or Elton John
25 Joni Mitchell, Brenda Lee or Carly Simon

C

In what year were the following born?
1   James Last and Ken Dodd
2   Prince and Michael Jackson
3   Boy George and Jimmy Somerville
4   Hazell Dean and Belinda Carlisle
5   Jason Donovan and Kylie Minogue
6   Kenny Rogers and Tina Turner
7   Bonnie Tyler and Cyndi Lauper
8   Lulu and Donna Summer
9   Yoko Ono and Nina Simone
10 Quincy Jones and Willie Nelson
11 Bob Dylan and Paul Simon
12 Kirsty MacColl and Irene Cara
13 Captain Sensible and David Lee Roth
14 Luther Vandross and Sting
15 Barry Manilow and Gilbert O'Sullivan
16 Paul Young and Nigel Kennedy
17 Ian Dury and Alvin Stardust
18 Engelbert Humperdinck and Glen Campbell
19 Cher and Dolly Parton
20 Kiki Dee and Emmylou Harris
21 Julian Lennon and Whitney Houston
22 Rick Astley and Lisa Stansfield
23 Robert Palmer and Billy Joel
24 Gary Numan and Paul Weller
25 Sinitta and Janet Jackson

4 Who Killed Bambi?

This is a quiz about animals on disc. There are bands named after animals, and songs about animals, to say nothing of the sounds of animals themselves on record. These questions test your knowledge.

A

1. Which Bunny launched his chart career with three number ones?
2. Which elephant "packed her trunk and said goodbye to the circus"?
3. 'The Lion Sleeps Tonight' was number one for which British group in 1982?
4. Which animal featured in two songs with the same title, which provided Top Five hits for Manfred Mann and Sweet?
5. Whose *Keep Your Distance* album included the hit singles 'Down To Earth' and 'Ordinary Day'?
6. Which superstar was 'Rat Rapping' in 1983?
7. 'Hotel California' was a hit single and album for which band?
8. Which British group of the Eighties scored their first Top Ten hit with 'Dog Eat Dog'?
9. 'Rabbit' was a 1980 Top Ten hit for which Cockney duo?
10. What stance was Neneh Cherry taking in 1988?
11. Whose first chart-topper was 'Tiger Feet'?
12. And whose first chart-topper was 'Eye Of The Tiger'?
13. Who hit number one with 'The Chicken Song'?
14. Who had a dog, and a hit single, called 'Jet'?
15. Whose second and comparatively unsuccessful album was called 'Neither Fish Nor Flesh'?
16. Whose first hit, in 1986, was called 'Digging Your Scene'?
17. Which band hit number one with the instrumental 'Albatross'?
18. Which hit by the Tweets spent 28 weeks on the chart from 1981?
19. Who was born Steven Georgiou in 1947 and hit with 'I Love My Dog' before he changed his name to Yusuf Islam in the late Seventies?
20. Which heavy metal band has a one-armed drummer?

B

1. 'The Love Cats' brought which UK group a Top Ten hit?
2. 'Rat Trap' was the first of two number ones for which Irish band?
3. Which animal featured in Madonna's 'Like A Virgin' video?
4. Who took Paul Anka's 'Puppy Love' to number one in 1972?
5. And which other teenybopper star of the Seventies had a chart-topper with 'The Puppy Song'?
6. 'Nothing's Gonna Stop Me Now' was the third Top Ten hit for which female vocalist?
7. Which animal appears on the covers of Aztec Camera's album *Love* and Mr Mister's album *Welcome To The Real World*? Is it a) a horse b) a cow or c) a tiger?

8   Which animal appears on the cover of Pink Floyd's *Atom Heart Mother*? Is it a) a horse, b) a cow or c) a tiger?

9   In what year was 'I'm A Believer' by the Monkees number one?

10 Who managed to 'Rock This Town' in 1981?

11 What did UB40 find in their kitchen in 1987?

12 Who spent six years on the album chart with *Bat Out Of Hell*?

13 Who produced Liza Minnelli's first ever hit single in 1989?

14 What was the true identity of Apollo C. Vermouth, who produced the Bonzo Dog Doo Dah Band's hit 'I'm the Urban Spaceman'?

15 Under what name have Siouxsie Sioux and Budgie had several hits?

16 With which band did Alan Price begin his chart career?

17 Which Beatle had a solo hit with 'Cold Turkey'?

18 Which insect did Val Doonican find elusive in 1966?

19 Which film about rabbits had Art Garfunkel's number one hit 'Bright Eyes' as its theme?

20 At the 1990 Brits, Mrs Thatcher admitted to liking a 1953 chart-topper which asked the price of a pet. Which pet?

1   What was Eve Boswell picking in 1955?

2   Who failed to take mother's advice in 1970, even though 'Mama Told Me Not To Come'?

3   The same group also hit with a song whose lyric began, "Jeremiah was a bullfrog, he was a good friend of mine". What was the title?

4   Who said 'Gimme Dat Banana' in 1977?

5   From which Duran Duran album did 'Union Of The Snake' come?

6   Which cowardly animal asked for 'Just One More Night' in 1978?

7   Who hit the Top Ten in 1956 with 'Bluebottle Blues'?

8   Who did the Beatles name themselves after?

9   Which talkative long-haired grunting Tibetan ox gave the Coasters a hit in 1958?

10 Who was 'Walking My Cat Named Dog' in 1966?

11 Which band had Annabella L'win as its lead vocalist?

12 With which group did Christine McVie first enjoy chart success?

13 And in which group did Eric Clapton begin his chart life?

14 Which chart-topping band first hit the charts with the question 'How Will The Wolf Survive?'?

15 Who hit with the instrumental 'Alley Cat Song' in 1963?

16 Which band scraped into the Top Fifty in 1987 with 'Beautiful Imbalance'?

17 What was A Flock Of Seagulls' first hit single?

18 Who, besides Pigbag, has had a hit single with 'Papa's Got A Brand New Pigbag'?

19 Which foursome had a hit album called *Hedgehog Sandwich*?

20 Of which band was Batty Bat a member?

5 If I Said You Had A Beautiful Body, Would You Hold It Against Me?

The body has held an enduring fascination for songwriters and performers across the history of the charts. How good is your biology?

A

Who had hits with the following songs?

1 'I'm So Beautiful'
2 'Oh Yes You're Beautiful'
3 'You're So Vain'
4 'I'm A Wonderful Thing Baby'
5 'Together We Are Beautiful'
6 'Beauty's Only Skin Deep'
7 'You Sexy Thing'
8 'Raunchy'
9 'Looks Looks Looks'
10 'You Wear It Well'
11 'U Got The Look'
12 'Sartorial Eloquence'
13 'Vanity Kills'
14 'So Macho'
15 'Muscles'
16 'Rugged And Mean, Butch And On Screen'
17 'The Good The Bad And The Ugly'
18 'Pretty In Pink'
19 'Desire'
20 'El Bimbo'

B

Insert the missing part of the body:

1 'My _____ Adored You'
2 '_____ Up'
3 'Lucky _____'
4 'Let Me Cry On Your _____'
5 'Perfect _____'
6 'Fattie _____'
7 'She's Got _____'
8 'Never Turn Your _____ On Mother Earth'
9 '_____ To The Bottle'
10 'Third _____ Left _____'
11 '_____ High (Grip Your _____ And Move)'

12 'Big _____ Strikes Again'
13 '_____ Over _____'
14 'Wear My Ring Around Your _____'
15 '_____ Of Glass'
16 'When The Girl In Your _____ Is The Girl In Your _____'
17 'Under Your _____'
18 'Losing My _____'
19 '_____ Deep In The Blues'
20 'Mistle _____ And Wine'

1 Who said hello to a new brunette?
2 What does P.Y.T. stand for?
3 What is the titular connection between Michael Jackson and the Human League?
4 Who according to Rod Stewart had more fun?
5 Who produced *Like A Virgin* for Madonna?
6 What suggestive song was number one in America for 10 weeks?
7 Which song was subtitled 'Rhythm 1 Lust'?
8 *Beauty Stab* was the follow-up to which highly successful album?
9 How was the Bad Mama Jama proportioned?
10 Whose final hit was '(She's) Sexy And 17'?

6 Detroit City

All the questions in this three-part quiz pertain to the pride of Detroit, Motown Records. The company, founded by Berry Gordy Jr, included several labels, most notably Motown, Tamla and Gordy. In Britain early releases were available on Oriole and then Stateside before Gordy set up his UK outlet, Tamla Motown. The Tamla was eventually dropped, leaving Motown as the UK label for all acts.

1 What was Stevie Wonder's only UK number one?
2 On what album did 'Mercy Mercy Me (The Ecology)' first appear?
3 Of what group was Mary Wilson a member?
4 Frederick Earl Long had a hit with 'Here Comes the Judge'. By what name was he better known?
5 Berry Gordy wrote what number one by Jackie Wilson?
6 What act had an American number one cover version of the Marvelettes' American number one 'Please Mr Postman'?
7 What Motown act had the second million-selling version of 'I Heard It Through The Grapevine'?
8 Who is the lead singer of the Four Tops?

9　Among the early Motown classics that did not chart in Britain was 'Heat Wave'. Who had the Grammy winning version?

10　What was Charlene's number one?

11　By what name is Diane Earle better known?

12　With what female partner did Marvin Gaye record 'The Onion Song'?

13　Of which group was Martha Reeves the lead singer?

14　Who had the number one of Smokey Robinson and Stevie Wonder's song 'Tears Of A Clown'?

15　What was Michael Jackson's first solo hit?

16　How many miles did Edwin Starr march in 1969?

17　Which group consisted of William King, Ronald LePread, Walter Orange, Lionel Richie and Milan Williams?

18　The Supremes had five consecutive US number ones in 1964–65. Who wrote and produced all of them?

19　For what film did Diana Ross earn an Oscar nomination as Best Actress?

20　Who had the original hit version of 'What Becomes Of The Brokenhearted' in 1966?

B

1　Who had the original hit version of 'He Was Really Sayin' Somethin'' in 1965?

2　Rod Stewart charted twice with remakes of what Motown original?

3　On what album did 'Three Times A Lady' originally appear?

4　What group had a Motown subsidiary label named after them?

5　What was the first UK number one on the Tamla Motown label?

6　Donnie Elbert charted with remakes of what two Motown songs?

7　Name the three Isley Brothers.

8　Who wrote and produced Eddie Murphy's million-seller 'Party All The Time'?

9　Madeline Bell had the original US Top Forty version of what Motown million-seller?

10　Berry Gordy wrote what number one by Brian Poole and the Tremeloes?

11　What female group was formed and produced by Rick James?

12　On what Motown subsidiary did 'Night' by Frankie Valli and the Four Seasons appear?

13　Which Motown artist recorded the original version of 'You've Made Me So Very Happy', a 1969 hit for Blood Sweat And Tears?

14　Which Motown act had the first million-selling version of 'I Heard It Through The Grapevine'?

15　Marv Johnson had an earlier and bigger hit than his Top Ten Tamla tune 'I'll Pick A Rose For My Rose'. What was it?

16　Motown is a portmanteau of what two words?

17　What orator charted in the United States on the Gordy label?

18　The theme song to what Brooke Shields film gave Motown a US number one?

19 Of which group was David Ruffin a lead singer?

20 Who had the US number one of Smokey Robinson's song 'My Guy'?

1 Stacy Lattisaw topped the US Black chart in 1990 on a duet with which male star?

2 What was the first Supremes single on which Diana Ross received lead billing?

3 Who was the DJ who assembled a collage of interviews, news reports and versions of 'What The World Needs Now Is Love' and 'Abraham Martin And John'?

4 With what female partner did Marvin Gaye record 'My Mistake (Was To Love You)'?

5 Of which group was Bobby Taylor leader?

6 Berry Gordy wrote what song recorded by the Beatles?

7 What US top three group consisted of Joe Harris, Billie Calvin and Brenda Evans?

8 What was the title of Stevie Wonder's first US number one album?

9 What nationality was R. Dean Taylor?

10 Diana Ross, Marvin Gaye, Smokey Robinson and Stevie Wonder got together to sing 'Pops, We Love You'. Who was Pops?

11 By what name is Mary Christine Brockert better known?

12 Which Motown star was once in a group called the Mynah Birds with Neil Young?

13 What was the first compilation album to top the UK LP chart?

14 What was the first group to have a greatest hits album reach number one?

15 On what album did 'Come See About Me' originally appear?

16 Who was the first UK female signing to the Motown group?

17 What artist was signed to Motown in the Eighties after repeated victories on a televised talent show?

18 When recording for a Motown subsidiary, who was Meatloaf's partner?

19 Which Jackson brothers were in the original Jackson Five?

20 Who had the US number one of Smokey Robinson's song 'My Girl'?

7 Brothers In Arms

The following quiz concerns brothers in groups. All you have to do is name the group the brothers are, or were, members of. We have omitted the family name if that is an integral part of the group's name.

1 Matt and Luke Goss

2 Don and Phil

3 Gary and Martin Kemp

4 Maurice, Robin and Barry Gibb

5   Jackie, Tito, Marlon, Jermaine and Michael
6   Jackie, Tito, Marlon, Randy and Michael
7   Mark and David Knopfler
8   Robert and Ronald Bell
9   Ray and Dave Davies
10   Ali and Robin Campbell
11   Brian, Carl and Dennis Wilson
12   Jordan and Jon Knight

B

1   Alan, Wayne, Merrill, Jay and Donny
2   Garry, Russell and Roger
3   Ron and Russell Mael
4   Paul and Ciaran Brennan
5   John and Damian O'Neill
6   Patrick and Gregory Kane
7   David and Steve Batt
8   Tim, Andy and Jon Farris
9   Maurice, Verdine and Fred White
10   Kelvin and Junior Grant
11   Boon and Phil Gould
12   Eddie and Alex

C

1   Maurice, Tonino and Jacques Baliardo
2   Shaun and Paul Ryder
3   Paddy and Martin McAloon
4   Chris and Eddy Amoo
5   Ali and Mike Score
6   Craig and Charlie Reid
7   Gary and Kit Clark
8   Con and Dec Cluskey
9   Richard and Steve Young
10   Richard and Tim Butler
11   Aaron, Arthur, Charles and Cyril
12   Ziggy and Steve

8 No Particular Place To Go

Everybody knows that the Beatles came from Liverpool and the Housemartins from Hull. This quiz tests your knowledge about geography in rock music.

A

1 For which country were the Band Aid and Live Aid appeals launched?
2 Whose 'American Pie' reached number two in 1972?
3 What was the title of Simple Minds' 1989 number one hit single?
4 'Massachusetts' was the first number one single for which British group, who hit the top for the fifth time 20 years later?
5 American band Toto sang about which continent in 1983?
6 Where were the Police walking in 1979?
7 Whose 'Fairytale Of New York' featured the voice of Kirsty MacColl?
8 From where did the Proclaimers' letter come in 1987?
9 'The Final Countdown' was number one for which Swedish rock group in 1986?
10 'Waterloo' was the first of many number ones for which group?
11 Which London street did Gerry Rafferty remix in 1990?
12 Who wrote the classic 'Memphis Tennessee'?
13 And who lived and died in Graceland in that city?
14 Whose hit album was called *Graceland*?
15 Who planted the ''A' Bomb In Wardour Street'?
16 Who went 'All Around The World' for a number one in 1989?
17 Where did Scott MacKenzie recommend everyone should wear some flowers in your hair, in the flower power summer of 1967?
18 Who recorded 'London Calling', voted the best album of the Eighties by *Rolling Stone* magazine, though it was recorded in 1979?
19 Which band, led by Mark Shaw, had a 1989 hit single and album called 'Big Area'?
20 Which Seventies tartan teen idols hit the top with 'Bye Bye Baby'?

B

1 'Chanson D'Amour' was number one for which American group?
2 From which country do Nana Mouskouri and Demis Roussos come?
3 Where was Madonna's 'Like A Virgin' video shot?
4 Having seen 'Kids In America' reach number two, Kim Wilde released another track three singles later which also featured a country in the title. Name the hit.
5 'Tahiti' was the tenth Top Ten hit for which British star?
6 Who had Top Five hits with 'Requiem' and 'London Nights' in 1989?
7 Who spent 'One Night In Bangkok' and 14 weeks in the chart in 1984?
8 How high did Ultravox's 'Vienna' climb in the singles charts?

9 'Hey Manhattan' was whose follow-up to 'The King Of Rock 'N' Roll'?

10 Who had a Top Ten hit with 'My One Temptation' in 1988?

11 Whose hit album *Storm Front* includes the single 'Leningrad'?

12 Where was Bonnie Tyler lost in 1976?

13 What is the nationality of Candy Dulfer, Yvonne Keeley and Ben Liebrand?

14 For which country did Nicole win the Eurovision Song Contest in 1982?

15 What is the home country of the Yellow Magic Orchestra and Kyu Sakamoto?

16 What was the title of the Simple Minds' EP featuring their version of 'Sign O' The Times'?

17 Who hit number one with 'Rivers Of Babylon'?

18 Which state's girls did the Beach Boys wish they all could be?

19 Who topped the charts with 'Don't Cry For Me Argentina' in 1977?

20 Where did Debbie Harry fancy a bit of French Kissin'?

1 Whose *Liverpool* album included the hit singles 'Warriors (Of The Wasteland)' and 'Watching The Wildlife'?

2 Who were "hearing only bad news on Radio Africa" in 1986?

3 Which cathedral brought the New Vaudeville Band down in 1966?

4 Which town's Chosen Few scored a Top Ten success with 'Footsee' in 1975?

5 Where did Horst Jankowski, the German pianist, take a musical walk in 1965?

6 'Ghosts', 'Cantonese Boy' and 'I Second That Emotion' were hits for which British group?

7 Which American sang about 'An English Country Garden' in 1962?

8 'For America' was a 1986 hit for Jackson Browne in the USA, but which group had a British Top Ten hit with that title in the same year?

9 Where did Sensational Alex Harvey Band hold their 1976 tea party?

10 'Wishful Thinking' gave which group their only Eighties Top Ten hit?

11 Who had an Eighties greatest hits album called *New York New York*?

12 On which label was Thomas Dolby's 'She Blinded Me With Science' released in Britain?

13 From where did Bruce Springsteen's least successful album send greetings?

14 And which state was the title of another Springsteen album?

15 Who introduced the 'European Female' to the Top Ten in 1983?

16 What is the home country of Neil Young and Robbie Robertson?

17 Who has had hits with 'Israel', 'Arabian Nights' and 'Song From The Edge Of The World'?

18 Who maintained that "England Swings like a pendulum do"?

19 Who hit with Woody Guthrie's 'Grand Coolie Dam' in 1958?

20 What is the home country of Mezzoforte and the Sugarcubes?

9 Dress You Up

Here's a test of your dress sense and your awareness of chart fashion. Who cares what we wear, and who sings about it?

A

1   'Donald Where's Your _____'
2   'Wherever I Lay My _____ That's My Home'
3   'Puss 'N _____'
4   'Hand In _____'
5   'Venus In Blue _____'
6   'Goody Two _____'
7   'Favourite _____'
8   '_____ Off To Larry'
9   'Who Wears These _____'
10 'Full Metal _____'
11 'Sadie's _____'
12 'Baggy _____'
13 'Smarty _____'
14 'These _____ Were Made For Walkin''
15 'Your _____'
16 'Don't Let Go The _____'
17 'Cuff Of My _____'
18 'Boogie _____'
19 'Velcro _____'
20 'Leap Up And Down (Wave Your _____ In The Air)'

B

What colour were the following items of apparel?
1   Elvis Presley's Suede Shoes
2   Elvis Costello's Shirt
3   Nick Heyward's Hat
4   Prince's Beret
5   David Bowie's Jeans
6   The Flee-Rekker's Jeans
7   The Wombles' Tie and Tails
8   Norman Brooks' Shirt and Tie
9   New Model Army's Coat
10 King Brother's Sports Coat
11 Westworld's Mac
12 John Barry's Stockings
13 Alvin Stardust's Dress
14 Harry Belafonte's Ribbons
15 Brian Hyland's Itsy Bitsy Teeny Weeny Polka Dot Bikini

Who had British hit singles with the following essential accessories? :

16 'Lipstick Powder And Paint'
17 'Baubles, Bangles And Beads'
18 'Handbags And Gladrags'
19 'Good Luck Charm'
20 'Sunglasses'

1 Who went from 'Rags To Riches'?
2 What were Ally's Army kitted out in?
3 'Judy In Disguise (With Glasses)' was based on the title of which Beatles track?
4 Who were 'Falling Apart At The Seams'?
5 Which brand of jeans did David Dundas sing about?
6 What did Timbuk 3 wear to shield them from the future's glare?
7 Who sang of a transvestite *Star Wars* character?
8 What was Reparata's only solo hit?
9 Whose washing machine needs repairing?
10 Which band wore a 'Badge'?
11 And who wore 'The Crown'?
12 Who went crazy for a 'Sharp Dressed Man'?
13 Which duo recorded 'After A Fashion'?
14 What was the first single from Bruce Springsteen's *Tunnel Of Love* album?
15 Who loved a 'Man In Uniform'?
16 And who sang about their female counterparts?
17 Where did Connie Francis find her best friend's Lipstick?
18 What did Roxy Music go to bed in?
19 Who created a New Fashion?
20 What did the Moody Blues spend their Nights In?

10 Cover Me

How well do you know your album covers? This quiz shows album covers or parts of album covers well-known and not so well-known and all you have to do is identify them.

1▶

2

3▶

◀4

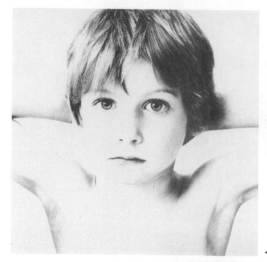

◀5

6▶

◀7

◀8

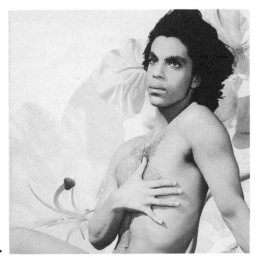

9▶

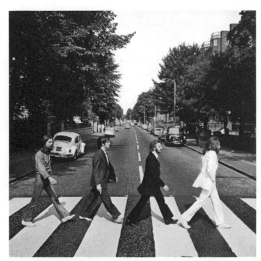

◀10

11▶

◀12

13▶

14▶

◀15

16▶

◀17

18▶

◀19

20▶

11 Put It There

Simply use the clues to add a letter to the names of various hitmakers to give them a whole new meaning. For example, if the clue was "Loud noise from Clapton, Bruce and Baker", the answer would be "Scream", which is Cream plus the letter S. The opposite to this quiz crops up later in the book (quiz 43 – The Letter).

A

1   Instruments used by Matt and Luke to sign cheques
2   Fresh tyremarks on the street are 'The Right Stuff'
3   David Byrne's group goes hunting
4   Small Ultravox vocalist
5   Neil and Chris make a nuisance of themselves
6   'Wuthering Heights' on ice
7   Austere childhood because 'Money's Too Tight To Mention'
8   Scandinavian Ascot essential
9   Marty's daughter throws stones across the water
10 Training shoe sponsorship for Tina and husband
11 Slow *Auf Wiedersehen Pet* star
12 Three steamrollered rappers
13 He left Stock Aitken Waterman to become a builder
14 What the Pearsons did in 1985
15 Breaking 4 Love causes a slight cut

B

1   Friendly first number one hitmaker
2   Bless you Mr Marvin
3   Adam's wife (a Wild Hearted Woman) gets enclosed
4   Ben Liebrand revives baby traffic gridlock
5   Scots Jesse gets mad
6   'Can't Get Enough' of Buster Bloodvessel, Errol Brown and Duncan Goodhew
7   Pete Wylie's great laundry
8   Gaping ravine for Rockney duo
9   Allergic to 'The Crunch'
10 'Rock Me Gently' and get in the mood
11 Iva Davies' Australian home for naughty ladies
12 Huey's amphibious backing band
13 Famous stupid rodent
14 Exact location of 'Storms In Africa'
15 'Low Rider' group get spotty

C

1 Mythical warrior rides a 'Little Donkey'
2 Make fun of a 'Male Stripper'
3 First tooth causes pain in a sensitive area but baby's 'Still Too Young To Remember'
4 Group in need of men in 'White Coats'
5 'I Can't Wait' for convent footwear
6 Audrey Hall's appetizing sister
7 The Kane brothers are big
8 Richie's house empire
9 'Tears' hitmaker takes an interest
10 Uncouth charity DJs
11 'Car Wash' group doesn't rhyme
12 Roy Wood's a film buff
13 Humiliating position for Jimmy Pursey
14 'Let My People Go Go' and become sewerage workers
15 Take the best-selling artist of the Thirties and Forties

12 Band On The Run

Can you remember when Craig Logan left Bros, or who replaced Pete Best in the Beatles? If you can't, then we don't fancy your chances in this quiz, which is about the many people who have moved from band to band during their careers.

A

1 Who moved from the Beatles to Wings?
2 Who moved from the Hollies to Crosby, Stills and Nash?
3 Who moved from Bronski Beat to the Communards?
4 Who moved from Blind Faith to Derek and the Dominoes?
5 Who moved from the Housemartins to Beats International?
6 Who moved from Japan to Sylvian Sakamoto?
7 Who moved from Yellow Magic Orchestra to Sylvian Sakamoto?
8 Who moved from the Faces to the Rolling Stones?
9 Which lady moved from the Tourists to Eurythmics?
10 Who moved from the Sex Pistols to Public Image Ltd?
11 Who moved from Jam to the Style Council?
12 Who moved from Yazoo to Erasure?
13 Who moved from the Beatles to the Traveling Wilburys?
14 Who moved from Soft Cell to Marc and the Mambas?
15 Who moved from Wham! to Boogie Box High?
16 Who moved from Deep Purple to Rainbow and back again?
17 Who moved from Rory Storme and the Hurricanes to the Beatles?
18 Who moved from Tom and Jerry to Simon and Garfunkel?
19 Who moved from Kandidate to Galaxy?
20 Who moved from the Specials to Terry, Blair and Anouchka?

B

1 Who moved from the Faces to the Who?
2 Who moved from Human League to Heaven 17?
3 Who moved from Band Aid to Band Aid II?
4 Who moved from King Crimson to Emerson, Lake and Palmer?
5 Who moved from Depeche Mode to Assembly?
6 Who moved from Chicken Shack to Fleetwood Mac?
7 Who moved from Manfred Mann to McGuinness Flint?
8 Who moved from Electric Light Orchestra to the Traveling Wilburys?
9 Who moved from Squeeze to Mike + the Mechanics?
10 Who moved from Generation X to Sigue Sigue Sputnik?
11 Who moved from the Modettes to the Communards?
12 Who moved from Slik to Ultravox?
13 Who moved from the Moody Blues to Wings?
14 Who moved from Hawkwind to Motorhead?
15 Who moved from the Smiths to Electronic?
16 Who moved from the Yardbirds to Led Zeppelin?
17 Who moved from the Spencer Davis Group to Blind Faith?
18 Who moved from the Big Three to the Mugwumps to the Mamas and the Papas?
19 Who moved from the Move to the Electric Light Orchestra to Wizzard?
20 Who moved from the Soft Machine to Police?

C

1 Who moved from Chic to the Honeydrippers?
2 Who moved from Roxy Music to Adam and the Ants?
3 Who moved from the New Christy Minstrels to the First Edition?
4 Who moved from the Mindbenders to Hotlegs?
5 Who moved from Culture Club to This Way Up?
6 Who moved from the Herd to Humble Pie?
7 Who moved from 10 C.C. to Wax?
8 Who moved from the Swinging Blue Jeans to the Hollies?
9 Who moved from Journey to Jefferson Starship?
10 Who moved from Johnny Kidd and the Pirates to the Tornados?
11 Who moved from the Idle Race to the Move?
12 Who moved from the Paramounts to Procol Harum?
13 Who moved from the Humblebums to Stealer's Wheel?
14 Who moved from Pride to Halo James?
15 Who moved from Cliff Bennett & the Rebel Rousers to the Searchers?
16 Who moved from Marty Wilde's Wildcats to the Shadows?
17 Who moved from Steampacket to the Faces?

18 Who moved from Patti LaBelle and the Bluebelles to the Supremes?
19 Who moved from the Ides Of March to Survivor?
20 Who moved from A Certain Ratio to Swing Out Sister?

13 Lady Madonna

Can you recognize these Madonna songs from just a few of the lyrics?

A

1 "You can dance – for inspiration"
2 "Everybody spread the word/We're gonna have a celebration all across the world"
3 "I want to be where the sun warms the sky/When it's time for siesta you can watch them go by"
4 "Only boys that save their pennies/Make my rainy day"
5 "Grace Kelly, Harlow Jean/Picture of a beauty queen"
6 "He says he's going to marry me/We can raise a little family/Maybe we'll be all right, it's a sacrifice"
7 "I close my eyes, Oh God I think I'm falling/Out of the sky"
8 "She's trouble in a word/Get closer to the fire, run faster/Her laughter burns you up inside"
9 "I've had other guys/I've looked into their eyes/But I never knew love before till you walked through my door"
10 "Come on shine your heavenly body tonight/'Cause I know you're gonna make everything all right"

B

1 "It doesn't matter if you win or lose/It's how you play the game so get into the groove"
2 "Oh your love thawed out/Yeah your love thawed out/What was scared and cold"
3 "All your suits are custom made in London/I've got something that you'll really like"
4 "Rub this magic lantern/He will make your dreams come true"
5 "I don't know why I thought that you could make me happy/These tears I cry for you are so hopeless"
6 "Long stem roses are the way to your heart, but/He needs to start with your head"
7 "If you want me let me know/Baby let it show/Honey don't you fool around"
8 "If you gave me half a chance you'd see/My desire burning inside of me/But you choose to look the other way"
9 "If I ran away I'd never have the strength/To go very far/How would they hear/The beating of my heart"
10 "I was never satisfied with casual encounters"

1 "Don't want to say this but I think that I should/I'm better off forgotten if you think that I'll be good"

2 "Can you feel the rhythm of my mind/Boy I've got so much to give/But I don't want to waste my time"

3 "All the books I've read/All the things I know/Never taught me to live/Never taught me to let go"

4 "I'm tired of sharing all the hand-me-downs/To get attention I must always be the clown"

5 "I can't hear the traffic rushing by/Just the pounding of my heart/And that's why"

6 "I can see you've been hurt before/But don't compare them to me/'Cause I can give you so much more"

7 "If there's a chance then I know I've got to try/I'll make him dance with me/I'll make him tell me why"

8 "Not demanding, for a man that's really quite rare/You're not the least bit obsessed with your hair"

9 "Oop shoo boop oop oop sha la la/Took my advice and got out of this place"

10 "If I can get to the weekend/Everything will work out just fine/That's when I can go crazy/That's when I can have fun"

14 The Politics Of Dancing

Music and politics have been intertwined since before King Henry VIII wrote 'Greensleeves'. In this quiz we test you out on political messages in hit records, the political activities of recording stars and the recording careers of the politicians.

1 Which ex-Beatle hit with 'Give Peace A Chance'?

2 Which ex-Beatle hit with 'Give Ireland Back To The Irish'?

3 Which ex-Beatle masterminded the Concert For Bangladesh?

4 Which ex-Beatle seems to have kept out of politics altogether?

5 Whose 'Nelson Mandela' song became a worldwide anthem in the late Eighties?

6 Which ex-Genesis vocalist wrote and hit with 'Biko'?

7 Which Genesis vocalist protested about homelessness in his hit, 'Another Day In Paradise'?

8 What was the average age of the American soldiers in Vietnam?

9 What act began their chart career with 'Anarchy In The UK?'

10 Whose 'God Save The Queen' hit number two despite an airplay ban?

11 Which Frankie Goes To Hollywood hit featured a video with actors portraying Presidents Reagan and Chernenko?

12 Who hit number one with 'Rubber Bullets'?

13 What was the title of Nicole's Eurovision winner in 1982?

14 Who hit with 'Election Day' in 1985?

15 And which other band, with the same lead vocalist, invited us to 'Meet El Presidente' in 1987?

16 Which Billy Bragg song gave Kirsty MacColl a Top Ten hit in 1985?

17 Which song about inner city deprivation brought Elvis Presley back into the Top Ten after a three-year gap?

18 What was the Specials' number one on the same theme?

19 What was Pink Floyd's chart-topping comment on education?

20 From which musical does the song 'Don't Cry For Me Argentina' come?

B

1 Who told the world in the Sixties that 'The Times They Are A-Changing'?

2 And which friend of his had the only British chart version of 'We Shall Overcome'?

3 Who charted with his catchy plea for 'No Clause 28'?

4 Who suggested 'Stand Down Margaret' in 1980? But she didn't.

5 What title was used by both Malcolm McLaren and Jeffrey Osborne for hit singles?

6 Who came to prominence at Nelson Mandela's 70th birthday party concert, playing her apolitical hit 'Fast Car'?

7 Who believed we were on 'The Eve Of Destruction' in 1965?

8 Who originally hit with 'War'?

9 Which band's name almost means 'Political Writings' in Italian?

10 Which 1980 number two hit included the line, "Peace has come to Zimbabwe"?

11 Who pleaded with us, 'Don't Drive Drunk' in 1984?

12 Whose guitar performance of 'The Star Spangled Banner' was one of the highlights of the Woodstock Festival?

13 Whose anti-Vietnam 'I Feel Like I'm Fixing To Die Rag' featuring the infamous 'Fish Cheer' also enlivened Woodstock?

14 Who hit with the almost political album, *No. 10 Upping St*?

15 Which band was proud to be 'Part Of The Union' in 1973?

16 Whose biggest solo hit in the Eighties was 'Russians'?

17 Whose albums include 'Worker's Playtime' and 'Talking With The Taxman About Poetry'?

18 What was Alice Cooper's follow-up to 'School's Out'?

19 Whose hits include 'White Riot' and 'This Is England'?

20 Who hit with the deeply political 'Santa Claus Is On The Dole'?

C

1 Who produced the Osmonds and went on to become Lieutenant Governor of California?

2 Who wrote 'It's All In The Game' and went on to become Vice-President of the United States?

3 Who was Miss X, whose hit 'Christine' in 1963 commented on the Profumo affair?

4 Which statesman had a posthumous hit album of speeches in 1965?

5 Which tasteless band first hit the chart with 'Kill The Poor'?

6 Who first hit with 'African And White'?

7 Who featured on 'Fool Britannia' (with Anthony Newley and Joan Collins) and 'How To Win An Election' (with Harry Secombe and Spike Milligan)?

8 Who had a Top Twenty album in 1981 called *Sandinista*?

9 Which black leader died on 21 February 1965, but hit the charts in 1984?

10 For what film did George Fenton and Jonas Gwangwa perform the title theme?

11 What was Dozy, Beaky, Mick and Tich's only hit without Dave Dee?

12 Who originally recorded 'Abraham Martin And John', which Marvin Gaye took to the Top Ten?

13 Which Greyhound hit gave Three Dog Night an American smash?

14 Whose first album was called *Thank Christ For The Bomb*?

15 What did the Council Collective's hit 'Soul Deep' raise money for?

16 What hit had the label and catalogue number Ensign BONGO 1?

17 Which band claimed in their publicity to have been held prisoner in Vietnam for almost 20 years?

18 Whose 1989 album was entitled *Protest Songs*?

19 Which album title connects the Eurythmics, Van Halen and Rick Wakeman?

20 Which reggae superstar performed at Zimbabwe's independence celebrations in 1980?

---

15 Coming Around Again

A large number of old records have been hitting the charts over the past few years, coming back to chart life for a variety of reasons. Can you remember these raves from the grave?

These hits were all resurrected by advertisers trying to sell their wares on television. Can you remember the goods they were aiming to sell?

1 'Stand By Me' – Ben E. King

2 'He Ain't Heavy He's My Brother' – Hollies

3 'I Can See Clearly Now' – Johnny Nash

4 'Take My Breath Away' – Berlin

5 'Lovely Day' – Bill Withers

6 'Move Over Darling' – Doris Day

7 'Easy' – Commodores

8 'Stop! In The Name Of Love' – Supremes

9 'Reach Out I'll Be There' – Four Tops

10 'Let's Stick Together' – Bryan Ferry

B

1 'Sailing' by Rod Stewart has re-entered the chart twice, each time for a different reason. What were those reasons?

2 In the Eighties, the entire Beatles singles catalogue was re-issued, but only one made the Top Ten. Which one?

3 Which three John Lennon hits made number one after his death?

4 Slade's 'Merry Xmas Everybody' was a Christmas hit seven times in the Eighties. In which years?

5 James Brown's 'I Got You' and Martha Reeves' 'Nowhere To Run' hit the chart again in 1988 after their inclusion in which film?

6 How many of Elvis Presley's singles returned to the chart in the immediate aftermath of his death?

7 'Let's Get Brutal' was a re-mixed hit for Nitro Deluxe in 1988. What was the original title?

8 Why was Rose Royce's 'Is It Love You're After' a hit again in 1988?

9 Who had 13 records re-enter the charts between 22 January and 5 February 1983?

10 Chaka Khan's hits were re-mixed and released on an album in 1989. What was it called?

C

It has been known for re-mix engineers to receive equal billing to that of the artist. The following were all hits again thanks to the talents of famous producers – who?

1 'The Eve Of The War' – Jeff Wayne

2 'The Time Warp' – Damian

3 'Downtown' – Petula Clark

4 'I Feel Love' – Donna Summer

5 'In The Air Tonight' – Phil Collins

6 'I'm Every Woman' – Chaka Khan

7 'You To Me Are Everything' – Real Thing

8 'I.O.U.' – Freeez

9 'Blue Monday' – New Order

10 'You Sexy Thing' – Hot Chocolate

16 Monkey

This is an acrostic. When filled in with the correct letters, the boxed area quotes the lyric of a hit single. The letter in the top left of each square refers you to the lettered clues. Answer the clues by filling in the boxes as the numbers indicate. When completed the first letters of clues A through to Z spell out the artist and title of the quoted song. AA gives you a further hint.

A She recorded 'Mercedes Boy'
74 141 122 153 134 26 96

B Christian name of quoted artist's former partner 68 7 40

C Jim Webb standard (4 words)
6 38 131 18 112 137 89 4 66 41 145

D After the quoted artist's 1980 hit? (4 words) 103 9 148 49 42 95 158 118 159 55 88 27 135 13 44 8 99

E A Jam number one 19 150 57 71 119

F '110 146 23 67 120 It Would Rain', hit by the Temptations (2 words)

G Tami Lynn and the Fascinations had a hit on this label 17 32 35 157

H 65 76 Well, group with eponymous hit

I Nancy 93 72 48 102, 1982 chart artist

J Public Enemy were experts on this in 1990 24 77 29 64 21 50

K Album by quoted artist (3 words) 69 129 136 10 75 3 116 61 106 142 123 126 94 46

L 152 111 20 60 and the Bunnymen

M '155 162 1 109 82 139 Eyes', 1979 number one

N Phil 79 91 128 86, Sixties folk and protest singer

O '30 36 87 51 73 107 (Gimme Some)', first Fatback Band hit (2 words)

P '90 58 26 140 104 117 138 To Be Humble', Mac Davis' biggest UK hit (2 words)

Q The Velvet Underground and 105 92 81 11

R Tina Turner Top Five hit, '2 151 70 130 160 115 22' (2 words)

S Joni Mitchell's last Top Fifteen album to date 63 53 15 125 56 108

T '121 97 78 163 124 Garden', Elton John tribute to John Lennon

U Sweet 1978 hit 144 161 133 34

V '12 80 127 100 52 149 43', Stevie Wonder's first British hit

W Neal had a Hefti hit with his theme 132 154 5 37 143 54

X Lene Lovich sang its song 31 114 84 14

Y 'Leather and 113 83 101 28', Stevie Nicks' US hit duet with Don Henley

Z '47 98 85 147 6', Yankovic parody (2 words)

AA For this song, this was in Johannesburg 39 45 16 33 59 156.

M (1)	R (2)	K (3)	C (4)	W (5)	C (6)	B (7)	D (8)	–	D (9)	K (10)	Q (11)	V (12)	D (13) X (14)

S (15) AA (16) G (17) C (18) | E (19) L (20) J (21) R (22)

F (23) J (24) P (25) | A (26) D (27) Y (28) J (29) O (30) X (31) G (32) AA (33) V (34) | G (35) O (36) W (37) C (38)

AA (39) B (40) C (41) D (42) V (43)

D (44) AA (45) K (46) | Z (47) I (48) D (49) J (50) O (51) | V (52) S (53) W (54) D (55) S (56) E (57) P (58) AA (59) L (60) K (61)

Z (62) S (63) J (64) H (65) C (66) F (67) | B (68) | K (69) R (70) E (71) I (72) | O (73) A (74)

K (75) H (76) J (77) | T (78) N (79) V (80) | Q (81) M (82) Y (83) X (84) Z (85) N (86)

O (87) D (88) C (89) P (90) N (91) Q (92) I (93) K (94) | D (95) A (96) | T (97) Z (98) D (99) V (100) Y (101) I (102) D (103)

P (104) Q (105) K (106) | O (107) S (108) M (109) F (110) L (111) C (112) Y (113) | X (114) R (115) | K (116) P (117) D (118)

E (119) F (120) T (121) | A (122) K (123) T (124) | S (125) K (126) | V (127) N (128) K (129)

R (130) C (131) W (132) U (133) A (134) D (135)

K (136) C (137) P (138) | M (139) P (140) A (141) | K (142) W (143) U (144) C (145) | F (146) Z (147) D (148) V (149)

E (150) R (151) L (152) | A (153) W (154) M (155) AA (156) G (157) D (158) | D (159) R (160) U (161) M (162) T (163)

17 The Name Of The Game

This one is self-explanatory. All you have to do is find the missing name in each case.

A

What surnames do these people have in common?

1 Delroy, Lorraine and Stedman
2 Matt and Luke
3 Freddie, Janet and Michael
4 Donny, Jimmy and Wayne
5 Sam, Joe and James
6 Barry, Andy and Robin
7 Quincy, Tom and Jimmy
8 Juggy, Rickie Lee and Grace
9 Jermaine, Joe and Millie
10 David, Eddie and Gogi
11 Chuck, Dave and Nick
12 Paul, Mark and Evelyn
13 Christian, Jimmy and Tommy
14 Kelly, Teena and Rose
15 Audrey, Pam and Terry
16 Glenn, Mitch and Roger
17 Willie, Sandy and Rick
18 Bernice, Ann, Maureen, Linda and Colleen
19 Marv, Holly and Johnny
20 Des, Hazel and Sinéad

B

What first names go with all of these surnames?

1 McCartney, Weller and Young
2 Michael, Harrison and McCrae
3 Bowie, Stewart and Gahan
4 Henley, McLean and Everly
5 Moore, Numan and Kemp
6 Harry, Gibson and Reynolds
7 Miller, Taylor and Hodgson
8 Hornsby, Willis and Springsteen
9 Ocean, Idol and Fury
10 Kelly, Jones and Slick
11 Jones, Petty and Robinson
12 Rea, De Burgh and Cross
13 Russell, Lee and Holloway
14 Wilde, Appleby and Carnes
15 Ronstadt, Womack and Scott

16 Chapman, Thorn and Ullman

17 Richards, Emerson and Harris

18 Bell, Stewart and Taylor

19 Rush, Holliday and Warnes

20 Brown, Jackson and Simon

C

What words are missing from these group and song titles?

1 Eon, Romance, Talking

2 Edition, Order, Kids On The Block

3 Mix II, My Name Is, Happy

4 Degrees, Fun Boy, Kayes

5 Roxanne, Thing, To Reel

6 Box, Simply, Sovine

7 Sheep, Dogs, Nun

8 Sugarhill, Kane, Of Four

9 Dancing, Laundry, Diana

10 Jones, Loves You, And Mary Chain

11 Crimson, Kurt, Sun D'Moet

12 Last, Rapping, Blue

13 Of Fun, Arrest, Nation

14 Long Tall, Don't You Grieve, Go Round The Roses

15 Know Much, Turn Around, You Want Me

16 Heart, Thing, Life, Times

17 Oh, Do Ya Love Me, Ocean

18 Remember Me, Reggae, Friendly

19 House Of, Seeds Of, Shack

20 I Don't Care, Jane, I Love Your Way

18 Everything Starts With An 'E'

This quiz is E-Zee. All the questions refer to songs, albums, labels or artists which begin with the letter E.

A

1 Who hit number one with 'Orinoco Flow' in 1988?

2 Who are Andy Bell and Vince Clarke?

3 What was EastEnder Nick Berry's only hit, a number one in 1986?

4 Who are David A. Stewart and Annie Lennox?

5 Who recorded the number one albums *Anything For You* and *Cuts Both Ways*?

6 Who duetted with Paul McCartney on his 1982 number one, 'Ebony And Ivory'?

7 Whose second number one album was called *Enjoy Yourself*?

8   What group name was used by Barney Sumner, Johnny Marr and Neil Tennant at the end of 1989?

9   Which band began their chart career with 'E=mc²'?

10 Who teamed up with Olivia Newton-John to hit number one with 'Xanadu' in 1980?

11 What was Kylie Minogue and Jason Donovan's number one hit duet?

12 Whose number ones include 'Temptation' and 'Cathy's Clown'?

13 Who recorded the number one album *Emotional Rescue*?

14 Which single brought Depeche Mode back to the Top Ten in 1990 after an absence of over five years?

15 Which ex-DJ hit the Top Ten in 1983 with 'Snot Rap'?

16 Which group's successes include 'Back Home' and 'This Time (We'll Get It Right)', although that time they didn't?

17 What song topped the charts by both Boy George and Ken Boothe?

18 Whose greatest hits album was called *Every Breath You Take*?

19 Who was the chart-topping drummer with Earth Wind and Fire?

20 And what was his number one called?

B

1   Who followed up their number one hit with 'Rock The Night' and 'Carrie'?

2   What was the name of the aircraft which carried the atom bomb to Hiroshima and became the title of an OMD hit?

3   Of which group was Ian McCulloch the lead vocalist?

4   Who hit number one in 1970 with 'I Hear You Knocking'?

5   Who is the leading solo instrumentalist in singles chart history?

6   Which group has Patsy Kensit as its lead vocalist?

7   Who strolled down 'Electric Avenue' in 1983?

8   And what Sixties chart-topping group did he play in?

9   Who took Rod Stewart's 'I Don't Want To Talk About It' back into the Top Ten in 1988?

10 Who hit the top with 'Hold Me Close'?

11 What Rupert Holmes hit was subtitled '(The Pina Colada Song)'?

12 Whose biggest UK hit was 'Hotel California'?

13 What was the only number one for Edison Lighthouse, in 1970?

14 Whose career was boosted first by Esther Rantzen and later by James Bond and Prince?

15 What was Survivor's number one hit?

16 What was the occupation of Ernie in Benny Hill's chart-topper?

17 Who hit with 'Friday On My Mind' in 1966?

18 Who did the Cramps date on their 1986 album?

19 Who won the FA Cup in 1985, and hit number 14 with their classic rendition of 'Here We Go'?

20 What was on the other side of the Beatles' 'Yellow Submarine'?

1   Who had the original hit version of 'The Clapping Song'?

2   Who duetted with Sarah Vaughan on 'Passing Strangers', a hit in both 1967 and 1969?

3   Who was Prince's drummer, who had her own hit with 'The Belle of St Mark' in 1985?

4   Who played with Dexy's Midnight Runners on 'Come On Eileen'?

5   From which Sixties group did Flash and the Pan emerge to hit the Top Ten in 1983?

6   On which label did the Boomtown Rats record their first ten hits?

7   What was the first record on the Epic label to top the UK charts?

8   Under what group name did an early Sex Pistols recording, 'Land Of Hope And Glory' hit the charts in 1985?

9   Who backed Johnny Cash on his 1972 Top Ten hit, 'A Thing Called Love'?

10 In which film did Cliff Richard sing 'A Voice In The Wilderness'?

11 Who duetted with Cliff Richard on the 1983 hit, 'She Means Nothing To Me'?

12 What was Elton John's tribute to John Lennon called?

13 Which Swiss band had a 1989 Top Ten hit borrowing heavily from Abba's 'S.O.S.'?

14 Which Barry Ryan hit did the Damned bring back to the Top Three in 1986?

15 Which US group couldn't stand the rain in 1978?

16 What was the 50th number one on the Columbia label, and to the start of 1990, the last instrumental to top the charts?

17 Who threatened to 'Kiss You All Over' in 1978?

18 Which ZZ Top album spent 135 weeks on the albums chart?

19 Who came back to the charts after 18 years' absence with 'Hello This Is Joanie (The Telephone Answering Machine Song)' in 1978?

20 Who had the first UK hit with Barrett Strong's classic 'Money'?

19 In a big country

This quiz takes us around the world in 50 questions.

Which country do the following acts come from?

A

1	Abba	11	Bryan Adams
2	Kylie Minogue	12	Vangelis
3	Sinéad O'Connor	13	Eddy Grant
4	Yello	14	Bob Marley
5	Technotronic	15	Kaoma
6	Black Box	16	Yoko Ono
7	Milli Vanilli	17	Sugarcubes
8	A-Ha	18	Freiheit
9	Julio Iglesias	19	Men At Work
10	Ofra Haza	20	U2

B

What was the nationality of the following items?

1	Don's Pie	12	The Passion's Film Star
2	Del's Maid	13	San Jose's Melody
3	David's Girl	14	Mantovani's Rhapsody
4	Grace's Guy	15	Jonathan's Reggae
5	Aneka's Boy	16	Frank's Foreign Legion
6	Aretha's Harlem	17	Andy's Soldier
7	Don's Reservation	18	The Pogues' and The Dubliners' Rover
8	Jimmie's Country Garden	19	Barry's Triangle
9	George's Love Affair	20	Eva's Trot
10	Steely Dan's Divorce		
11	Joe's Washerwoman		

C

Ten trick questions with a foreign flavour:

1 Which country did Vicky Leandros represent in the 1972 Eurovision Song Contest?

2 What is the only number one sung entirely in French?

3 Daniele Davoli had three hits in 1989 under which pseudonyms?

4 Who is Johann Holzel?

5 Where is Joan Armatrading from?

6 What was the title of Billy Joel's Live In Leningrad album?

7 Which two acts have won the Eurovision Song Contest for Israel?

8 When did Madness travel to Egypt by sea?

9 What nationality is Basia Trzetrzleweska and of which group was she a member?

10 Which hit was originally titled 'Ue Wo Muite Aruko' but was retitled with the name of a meat dish to hit the British and American charts?

20 The Road To Nowhere

There are those connections in rock music which are obvious and those that are sometimes more surprising and obscure. In this quiz we follow three chains of connections between people, songs and sounds, which lead nowhere except to prove, as Dean Martin showed in his heavy metal classic of 1964, everybody loves somebody sometime.

Explain what connects:

Sandie Shaw to the Smiths: the Smiths to Electronic: Electronic to the Pet Shop Boys: the Pet Shop Boys to Dusty Springfield: Dusty Springfield to Mike Hurst: Mike Hurst to 'The Mighty Quinn': 'The Mighty Quinn' to 'All I Really Want To Do': 'All I Really Want To Do' to Cher: Cher to Meatloaf: Meatloaf to Jim Steinman: Jim Steinman to Bonnie Tyler: Bonnie Tyler to Shakin' Stevens: Shakin' Stevens to Gary Glitter: Gary Glitter to Mike Leander: Mike Leander to Tom Jones: Tom Jones to Prince: Prince to Chaka Khan: Chaka Khan to Ray Charles: Ray Charles to the Blues Brothers: the Blues Brothers to Jive Bunny

B

Let's go from:

Sandie Shaw to Adam Faith: Adam Faith to David Essex: David Essex to Sinitta: Sinitta to Robert Knight: Robert Knight to the Love Affair: Love Affair to Mike Smith: Mike Smith to Marmalade: Marmalade to the Beatles: Beatles to Paul McCartney: Paul McCartney to Michael Jackson: Michael Jackson to Diana Ross: Diana Ross to Marvin Gaye: Marvin Gaye to Mary Wells: Mary Wells to Amii Stewart and Johnny Bristol: Johnny Bristol to the Osmonds: Osmonds to Mike Curb: Mike Curb to Clint Eastwood: Clint Eastwood to Lee Marvin

C

Try and find the way from:

Marianne Faithfull to Mick Jagger: Mick Jagger to Ron Wood: Ron Wood to the Faces: the Faces to Rod Stewart: Rod Stewart to B.A. Robertson: B.A. Robertson to Abba: Abba to Sandie Shaw: Sandie Shaw to Dionne Warwick: Dionne Warwick to Elton John: Elton John to Cliff Richard: Cliff Richard to Sarah Brightman: Sarah Brightman to Jimmy Somerville: Jimmy Somerville to Donna Summer: Donna Summer to Stock Aitken Waterman: Stock Aitken Waterman to Bananarama: Bananarama to Fun Boy Three: Fun Boy Three to Specials: Specials to Nelson Mandela: Nelson Mandela to Tracy Chapman

21 Girl Crazy

A little quiz about the ladies of rock. It is up to you to name names.

A

Who had number one hits with songs about these women?

1	Eileen	11	Annie
2	Lucille	12	Josephine
3	Mary	13	Michelle
4	Diana	14	Claudette
5	Diane	15	Clair
6	Cathy	16	Rose Marie
7	Julie	17	Grace
8	Juliet	18	Laura
9	Maggie May	19	Billie Jean
10	Lily	20	Yoko

B

The missing words in these song titles are all girls' names. Find them:

1 '_____'s A Singer'
2 '_____ The Midget (The Queen Of The Blues)'
3 'Oh _____ (Don't Feel Sorry For Loverboy)'
4 'It's Up To You _____'
5 '_____ (Ciao Baby)'
6 'All For _____'
7 'The Ballad Of _____ And Clyde'
8 'My Sweet _____'
9 '_____ Beware Of The Devil'
10 'Help Me _____'
11 'Dream Of _____'
12 '_____ Take A Bow'
13 'I Saw _____ Yesterday'
14 'Hello This Is _____ (The Telephone Answering Song)'
15 'Come Back _____'
16 '_____ Davis Eyes'
17 'Story Of _____'
18 'Hi Hi _____'
19 'Wait For Me _____'
20 '_____ Says Knock You In The Head'

C Which girls have each of the two acts in the questions had hits about? They are not necessarily the same song, just the same name somewhere in the title.

1 Marc Almond and the Rolling Stones
2 Cure and Julian Cope
3 Squeeze and Kid Creole
4 Ram Jam and Lonnie Donegan
5 Faces and Shane Fenton
6 Grapefruit and Tom Jones
7 Cliff Richard and Europe
8 Creedence Clearwater Revival and Danny Wilson
9 Lloyd Cole and the Hollies
10 AC/DC and Neil Diamond
11 Pogues and Little Richard
12 Elvis Presley and Cliff Richard
13 Racey and Johnny Cash
14 Four Tops and Anne Shelton
15 Slade and Jefferson Starship
16 Eddy Grant and Kool and the Gang
17 Mud and Marianne Faithfull
18 10 C.C. and Barry Manilow
19 Smokie and Full Force
20 All About Eve and Adam Faith

22 One Two Three O'Leary

How's your album collection? This quiz is designed to test your knowledge of the biggest hit albums, which every fan ought to have in their collection. We give you three tracks from the album, and you have to come up with the name of the album and the artist. None of them, incidentally, is a greatest hits collection. Half points for getting the artist only.

A
1 'Shout', 'Everybody Wants To Rule The World', 'I Believe'
2 'Shopping', 'Rent', 'It's A Sin'
3 'The Way You Make Me Feel', 'Liberian Girl', 'Dirty Diana'
4 'Fast Car', 'Across The Lines', 'Behind The Wall'
5 'It's Only Love', 'You've Got It', 'If You Don't Know Me By Now'
6 'The Loco-motion', 'It's No Secret', 'I'll Still Be Loving You'
7 'Helter Skelter', 'All Along The Watchtower', 'Angel Of Harlem'
8 'Share A Dream', 'The Best Of Me', 'Just Don't Have The Heart'
9 'I Remember When', 'Hold On', 'You Got It (The Right Stuff)'
10 'Black Boys On Mopeds', 'Nothing Compares 2 U', 'Three Babies'
11 'The Boy In The Bubble', 'Gumboots', 'You Can Call Me Al'

12 'King And Queen Of America', 'Sylvia', 'You Hurt Me (And I Hate You)'
13 'With A Little Help From My Friends', 'When I'm 64', 'Lovely Rita'
14 'The Eve Of The War', 'Forever Autumn', 'Brave New World'
15 'So Far Away', 'Walk Of Life', 'One World'
16 'I Wish It Would Rain Down', 'Another Day In Paradise', 'Colours'
17 'Baby Be Mine', 'Beat It', 'The Lady In My Life'
18 'All Around The World', 'This Is The Right Time', 'Mighty Love'
19 'Guns In The Sky', 'Need You Tonight', 'Mystify'
20 'Express Yourself', 'Cherish', 'Oh Father'

B

1 'Ordinary Day', 'Curiosity Killed The Cat', 'Shallow Memory'
2 'My Own Way', 'Hungry Like The Wolf', 'The Chauffeur'
3 'Something About You', 'Leaving Me Now', 'I Sleep On My Heart'
4 'Woman In Chains', 'Swords And Knives', 'Famous Last Words'
5 'Love Train', 'S.U.C.C.E.S.S.', 'Got It Made'
6 'Circle In The Sand', 'I Get Weak', 'Fool For Love'
7 'If You're Tarzan I'm Jane', 'I Feel The Earth Move', 'Water'
8 'Heart And Soul', 'Sex Machine', 'Valentine'
9 'A Smile In A Whisper', 'Find My Love', 'Fairground Attraction'
10 'You Keep It All In', 'From Under The Covers', 'I Love You (But You're Boring)'
11 'Steamy Windows', 'Undercover Agent For The Blues', 'Not Enough Romance'
12 'Handle With Care', 'Dirty World', 'End Of The Line'
13 'Michelle', 'I'm Looking Through You', 'If I Needed Someone'
14 'Up The Hill Backwards', 'Fashion', 'Ashes To Ashes'
15 'Telegraph Road', 'Private Investigations', 'It Never Rains'
16 'Go Your Own Way', 'You Make Loving Fun', 'Oh Daddy'
17 'Say Say Say', 'Tug Of Peace', 'Hey Hey'
18 'Material Girl', 'Shoo-Bee-Doo', 'Dress You Up'
19 'Se La', 'Love Will Conquer All', 'Say You Say Me'
20 'The Boxer', 'Baby Driver', 'The Only Living Boy In New York'

C

1 'Shattered Dreams', 'I Don't Want To Be A Hero', 'Foolish Heart'
2 'One And One', 'How Men Are', 'Paradise'
3 'Be My Twin', 'He Ain't No Competition', 'King Of Blue'
4 'Hello Hopeville', 'Graffiti Limbo', 'Anchorage'
5 'Secret Garden', 'I'll Be Good To You', 'I Don't Go For That'
6 'I Still Miss Someone (Blue Eyes)', 'Ooh My Love', 'Rooms On Fire'
7 'Like A Rolling Stone', 'Ballad Of A Thin Man', 'Desolation Row'
8 'Let Him Dangle', 'Veronica', 'Any King's Shilling'
9 'Anna (Go To Him)', 'Boys', 'P.S. I Love You'

10   'Stealin' Time', 'Baker Street', 'Right Down The Line'

11   'Wouldn't It Be Nice', 'Sloop John B', 'Caroline No'

12   'Too Much Heaven', 'Tragedy', 'Stop (Think Again)'

13   'The Man With The Child In His Eyes', 'Feel It', 'Room For The Life'

14   'Travelin' Band', 'Up Around The Bend', 'I Heard It Through The Grapevine'

15   'Nikita', 'Wrap Her Up', 'Candy By The Pound'

16   'So Lonely', 'Roxanne', 'Born In The 1950s'

17   'Milkcow Blues Boogie', 'Good Rockin' Tonight', 'Blue Moon of Kentucky'

18   'Mustapha', 'Fat Bottomed Girls', 'Don't Stop Me Now'

19   'Start Me Up', 'Neighbours', 'Waiting On A Friend'

20   'Blue', 'Just Making Memories', 'Sweetest Smile'

---

23 Time (Clock Of The Heart)

Time, measured in seconds, minutes, days, weeks, months and years, is an important element in music. Dance records are rated in beats per minute, the charts are updated each week and Max Bygraves has a chart career spanning 37 years. How much do you know about music and time?

---

1   'I Don't Like Mondays' was the second number one for which Irish group?

2   Which American vocalist accompanied Cherelle on her Top Ten hit, 'Saturday Love'?

3   How long did Silver Bullet give us to comply in 1990?

4   'Manic Monday' was a Top Five hit for which female group in 1986?

5   Whose 'Step On' brought them chart success in 1990?

6   Whose 'Blue Monday' dominated the Indie charts in the Eighties?

7   '1999' was a hit for whom in 1985?

8   Which group spent 'A Night At The Opera' and 'A Day At The Races' in the Seventies?

9   'Find The Time' and 'Another Weekend' were hits for which family group?

10   From which Bros album does 'Too Much' come?

11   'Sunday Girl' was the second of five number ones for which group headed by Debbie Harry?

12   Who made it 'A Night To Remember' in 1982?

13   'Doctorin' The Tardis' was a number one for which British group?

14   Which female vocalist scored her second Top Ten success in 1984 with 'Time After Time'?

15   Who saw 'In The Air Tonight' climb to number two in 1981 and the remix reach number four seven years later?

16   The Eurythmics' 'Sexcrime' was featured in which film?

17 Whose *Streetfighting Years* album includes the hits 'This Is Your Land' and 'Kick It In'?

18 Who had a UK Top Five hit with '9 to 5' in 1980?

19 *Decade* is the title of which group's greatest hits album?

20 'The Last Time' and 'Ruby Tuesday' were number one and number three hits respectively for which group in the Sixties?

B

1 'New Moon On Monday' was a Top Ten hit for which group in 1984?

2 Which female singer, formerly of Clannad, released 'Evening Falls . . .' as the follow-up to a number one hit?

3 Who just missed the Top Ten in 1984 with '2 Minutes to Midnight'?

4 Who was only '24 Hours From Tulsa' in 1963?

5 'Hourglass' was a Top Twenty hit for which group in 1987?

6 'Eight Days A Week' came from which Beatles album?

7 'Day After Day' was the third consecutive hit for which British group, the other two being 'Come And Get It' and 'No Matter What'?

8 From which musical does Damian's 'Time Warp' come?

9 Elvis Presley's 'I Got Stung' topped the charts as a double A-sided single with which other track?

10 Who was 'Counting Every Minute' in 1990?

11 Kool And The Gang, Shirley Bassey, David Bowie, and Move have all had hits with tracks called 'Tonight', but which of these four acts has achieved the highest chart position with the title?

12 'Nights In White Satin' charted in 1967, 1972 and again in 1979 for which British group?

13 Name Pilot's only number one.

14 'Showing Out (Get Fresh At The Weekend)' was which act's first hit?

15 Which football team had a Top Five hit with 'This Time (We'll Get It Right)' in 1982?

16 Whose 'Queen Of The New Year' charted at the beginning of 1990?

17 'Last Night I Dreamt That Somebody Loved Me' was the last hit for which group?

18 Who first hit the chart with 'Eighth Day' in 1980?

19 'The Time Has Come' was the seventh Top Five hit for which male singer in 1961?

20 Who had a number one hit album with *Only Yesterday*?

C

1 Who hit the Top Ten with their only hit, 'Love Like A Man' in 1970?

2 Who hit the Top Ten with 'April Skies' in 1987?

3 Whose *Midnight To Midnight* LP reached number 12 in 1987?

4 'Afternoon Delight' was a Top Twenty hit for whom in 1976?

5 In what year did T. Rex's '20th Century Boy' hit the Top Five?

6 Where did Showaddywaddy spend 'a night at' in 1979?

7 Who were 'Yesterday's Men' in 1985?

8 Chris Farlowe and The Rolling Stones both had hits with 'Out Of Time', but can you name the third artist to do so?

9 Who was the lead singer on Mike + The Mechanics' smash hit 'The Living Years'?

10 Who spent 'A Night In New York' in 1984?

11 Whose 'Morning Dance' hit the Top Twenty in 1979?

12 Where, according to the song, were Londonbeat at 9 a.m.?

13 Who felt that 'Time Drags By' in 1966?

14 Who scored her third Top Twenty success with 'January February' in 1980?

15 Which multiple Grammy award winner had a 1990 US number one album called *Nick Of Time*?

16 Whose *Reading, Writing And Arithmetic* album brushed the charts in 1990?

17 Which group crept up the charts with 'Half A Minute' in 1984?

18 Who wrote Kirsty MacColl's 1989 success 'Days'?

19 Which song was a hit for P. P. Arnold in 1968, for Mary Mason in 1977 and for Juice Newton in 1981?

20 Whose only chart success to date is 'The Calendar Song' which peaked at number 34 in 1977?

24 American Pie

All the questions in this quiz pertain to records that reached number one in the United States. Some questions are based on information in the *Billboard Book Of Number One Hits* by Joel Whitburn, published in Britain by Guinness Publishing.

1 George Michael took four number ones off which album?

2 The Beatles got to number one with all but which of the following: a) 'Hey Jude', b) 'She Loves You', c) 'Let It Be' or d) 'My Bonnie'?

3 'Rock Around The Clock' by Bill Haley and his group is considered the first number one of the rock era. What was the name of his group?

4 What father and daughter act had a number one?

5 What number one by Diana Ross had originally been recorded by Marvin Gaye and Tammi Terrell?

6 Who was John Travolta's singing partner on 'You're The One That I Want'?

7 With which two artists did Barbra Streisand have number one duets?

8 What number one had the subtitle 'Take A Look At Me Now'?

9 What was Debbie Reynolds' number one from the film *Tammy And The Bachelor*?

10 The Beatles had 20 American number ones. What was the first?

11 What vocalist from the group Chicago had a solo number one?

12 What was the charity number one by USA For Africa?

13 What 1983 British number one took five years to get to number one in America?

14 Who wrote Rick Astley's 'Never Gonna Give You Up'?

15 Who had the number one version of 'La Bamba'?

16 Who, in 1986, was the second Austrian to have a number one?

17 With which two American stars did Paul McCartney have number one duets?

18 What number one by The Doors did not make the British chart?

19 Who recorded 'Where Broken Hearts Go'?

20 Who were the friends in 'That's What Friends Are For' by Dionne Warwick and Friends?

B

1 What brother of David Cassidy had a number one?

2 What number one had the subtitle 'No More Love On The Run'?

3 Who was Phil Collins' singing partner on 'Separate Lives'?

4 Elvis Presley had a double-sided number one in 1956, 'Don't Be Cruel' and: a) 'Heartbreak Hotel', b) 'Blue Suede Shoes', c) 'Hound Dog' or d) 'Love Me Tender'?

5 'Nel Blu Dipinto Di Blu' is better known by its subtitle. What is the subtitle?

6 Why was the 1957 Christmas number one by Pat Boone strangely timed?

7 What was Michael Jackson's first US number one?

8 The film *Blue Velvet* contained the number one version of the title song by what artist?

9 What was Little Stevie Wonder's first number one?

10 Which of these artists had a number one single: a) Bob Dylan, b) The Who, c) Lorne Greene or d) Joni Mitchell?

11 The number one version of 'Na Na Hey Hey Kiss Him Goodbye' was by whom?

12 Though less famous than 'You've Lost That Lovin' Feeling', the Righteous Brothers did have a longer running number one. What was it?

13 What is the only record to go to number one in two different chart runs?

14 Which ex-Beatle had a number one in 1988?

15 Who had the number one version of 'Mony Mony'?

16 Who wrote the Crystals' 'He's A Rebel'?

17 With which two men did Jennifer Warnes have number one duets?

18 'Lost In Emotion' and 'Head To Toe' were 1987 number ones for whom?

19 The theme from which film gave Percy Faith nine weeks at number one?

20 What was Abba's only US number one?

C

1 What is the only US state named in the titles of three number ones?

2 Which was an American number one for Elvis Presley: a) 'A Big Hunk O' Love', b) 'Wooden Heart', c) 'Return To Sender' or d) 'Wear My Ring Around Your Neck'?

3 Who was the only Japanese artist to top the American chart?

4　Which Kris Kristoffersen song by which artist got to number one?

5　Paul and Linda McCartney had a number one that was never released as a single in the UK. What was it?

6　'TSOP' was a number one by MFSB. What do the act's initials stand for?

7　What Los Angeles DJ had a number one?

8　What was Fleetwood Mac's only American number one single?

9　Steve Greenberg was the producer of what disco smash?

10　Which number one had the subtitle 'Forget About Me'?

11　What was Billy Vera's group?

12　Who had the number one version of 'The Green Door'?

13　Rhythm Heritage had a number one theme from which TV series?

14　What was the title of Bill Conti's theme from *Rocky*?

15　What were the two number one singles from *Flashdance*?

16　On what John Lennon number one does the Plastic Ono Nuclear Band receive credit?

17　Where was Paul McCartney and Wings' live version of 'Coming Up' recorded?

18　Who, in 1950, was the first Austrian to have a number one?

19　Which James Bond theme was a number one?

20　Which three artists had number ones called 'Venus'?

25　Cross The Track (We Better Go Back)

This is a crossword, in two parts which make up the shape of '89. The clues refer to the music of that year.

EIGHT

Across

3　Billy, who stormed back into the charts (4)

4　Former Clannad keyboardist who made her Watermark (4)

6　Second half of a Norwegian trio (2)

8　Sorry, said Liza (2)

10　How Jimmy Somerville said goodbye in French (7)

12　Stylish outfit who hit with Italo House Mix (6)

13　Meat_____ (4)

15　Miss June Kingston and also Mr Hunt of the Wonder Stuff (5)

17　(and 11 down) _____ _____ Soul (2,2)

18　The noisy cry from Mahlathini (4)

20　(see 39 down)

22　Italian Rhythms practised by Sueno and Gloria Estefan (6)

23　These days were good for Gun (6)

26　Steve, who was going down with Aerosmith (5)

27　What the FPI Project were In Paradise (4)

28　Who Too Are One (2)

29　Gloria's on her own now (7)

31 Mr King, whose debut came with 55 down (1,1)

32 Mix, Entry or Issue (2)

33 _____ Gone _____ (4,3)

34 Label that houses Norman Cook and Billy Bragg (2)

35 (and 41 down) Edie Brickell's debut hit (4,1,2)

38 Perpetrators of 'A Great Radio Controversy' (5)

40 Baby Ford started the year nonsensically (6)

42 'Let Me Love You For Tonight' kicked off her career (6)

44 Mick's band lit a new one, the Bangles' was Eternal (5)

45 What according to the Funky Worm equalled love (1,1,2)

47 'Oye _____ Canto' (2)

48 Swedish lady who got a Top Ten hit (5)

50 Guns N' Roses album was full of them (4)

52 Donny is one (6)

54 Bros have had enough (3,4)

56 How Eddy goes up and down and Gets Funky (2)

57 Isn't, Wasn't, Ain't Never Gonna Be (2)

58 It's over now for Ultra (4)

59 Brother Beyond doubled up (4)

Down

1 Debut album for a Housemartins spin-off (7,2,3,9,5)

2 Yes, they did reform this year (8,7,7,4)

3 Mythological character who scored two number ones (5)

5 Number one artist who left the SAW stable (6)

7 They Toughed It Out (2)

9 'Say _____ Go' (2)

11 (see 17 across)

12 Noble House hitmakers who scored with 'Yeah! Buddy' (5)

14 Where 25 down wanted to go (5)

16 _____ The War (5)

19 What Pop Will do to Itself (3)

21 How much Queen wanted (3)

24 Where Love Came To (4)

25 (and 33 down) DJ who was solid, but a push over (2,4)

30 What Alyson did in her sleep (4)

33 (see 25 down)

36 How many times Phil urged us to think (5)

37 The Well that covered Fleetwood Mac (2)

39 (and 20 across) Beatmasters' double 'A' that was largely ignored (3,5)

40 The summer was too hot for Bananarama, Bobby didn't like it either (5)

41 (see 34 across)

43 Reggae band who have gone On And On (5)

46 Surname of a star, back after a seven-year hiatus thanks to Prince (6)

49 Tony, who this year produced Paul Johnson and Kim Wilde, but is better known for his work with Bananarama (5)

51 'Room _____ Your Heart' (2)

53 '_____ Only I Could' (2)

55 Best-selling Irish band ever (2)

NINE

Across

1 Arthur who earns his bread with the Backbeat Disciples (5)

5 Mr Sure or Mr Green (2)

6 Soft Metal band who were there for you (3,4)

8 Band that includes Ringo Starr's son on drums (1,1,1,1)

9 God? (4,7)

13 Grace Jones look-alike who commanded 'Respect' (5)

14 What Kon Kan did (3)

15 Early Eighties band that popped 'Up' again (1,1,1)

16 'Straight Up' Paula (5)

18 Where Wendy and Lisa's fruit was to be found (2,3,6)

20 Welsh rockers clocked two hits (5)

21 The Assault to be Handled With Care (7)

25 Lady who hit with a track by 7 down (4)

27 Second half of a group that 'Fell In And Out Of Love' (6)

28 Jason had too many broken ones (6)

30 The part of the City where 'Good Times' and 'Big Fun' can be had (5)

31 Two-thirds of a damp band (3,3)

34 Group led by Bret Michaels (6)

38 Small mammal that liked to Swing and Party (4,5)

39 Spanish artist who sang about another (7)

Down

1 Mr Liebrand, 'Eve Of The War' re-mixer (3)

2 Propagators of the 'Lambada' (5)

3 David Byrne's album: _____ Momo (3)

4 Comic Relief sextet (10,2,2,3,3,3,3)

6 '_____ _____ _____ Down' – Jesus Jones (5,2,2)

7 Frankie Beverley's group have been difficult to find (4)

10 Fairground Attraction's girl (5)

11 'That's What I Like' was built around this dance (5)

12 Where U2's Angel hailed from (6)

17 Hazell _____ (4)

19 Alexander, who regularly hit the singles chart with tracks from a two-year-old album (5)

22 Bronski Beat and Eartha Kitt shared two cups of tea (3)

23 Shakespear's Sister did it silently, New Order did 2 (3)

24 Gianfranco Bortolotti's San Franciscan football team (5)

26 Johnny, who went from the Smiths to Electronic (4)

29 He Turned Up The Bass (5)

32 They Are Sexual Perverts (1,1,1,1)

33 Soul II Soul's record label (3)

35 What was lurking beneath Bette's Wings (4)

36 'You'll Never Stop _____ Loving You' (2)

37 What Cher wanted to do with time (4)

26 Two Out Of Three Ain't Bad

In the sections below A1, B1 and C1, and so on, are all by the same artist. In Section A we list the more obscure singles that you may only recognize if you are a real fan. Score three points if you can guess the artist at this particular stage. If you find A too difficult, Section B will list something a little better known: score two points if you name the act here. If you need the third clue, score only one.

A

1 'Rules Of The Game'
2 'Let's Go To Bed'
3 'Paradise'
4 'Another Night'
5 'Purgatory'
6 'Call Out The Dogs'
7 'That Joke Isn't Funny Anymore'
8 'Family Man'
9 'I Wanna Be Your Lover'
10 'I've Got Mine'
11 'The Woman In Me'
12 'Never Gonna Cry Again'
13 'The Dreaming'
14 'Que Sera'
15 'Life In A Day'
16 'Tokyo Storm Warning'
17 'Song From The Edge Of The World'
18 'Thrown Away'
19 'Hungry Heart'
20 'Where Do We Go From Here'

B

1 'Run For Your Life'
2 'Lovesong'
3 'Muscles'
4 'Think'
5 'The Number Of The Beast'
6 'White Boys And Heroes'
7 'Last Night I Dreamt That Somebody Loved Me'
8 'Dreams'
9 'Glam Slam'
10 'Maybe Tomorrow'
11 'Love Is In Control (Finger On The Trigger)'
12 'Would I Lie To You'
13 'The Big Sky'
14 'Stainsby Girls'
15 'Ghostdancing'
16 'Pump It Up'
17 'Fire Works'
18 'Skin Deep'
19 'Spare Parts'
20 'Baby You're Dynamite'

C

1 'The Land Of Make Believe'
2 'The Love Cats'
3 'Chain Reaction'
4 'Respect'
5 'The Evil That Men Do'
6 'Are "Friends" Electric'
7 'Heaven Knows I'm Miserable Now'
8 'Everywhere'
9 'Purple Rain'

10 'Red Red Wine'
11 'I Feel Love'
12 'Sweet Dreams (Are Made Of This)'
13 'Wuthering Heights'
14 'The Road To Hell'
15 'Don't You (Forget About Me)'
16 'Oliver's Army'
17 'Hong Kong Garden'
18 'Golden Brown'
19 'Born To Run'
20 'We Don't Talk Anymore'

27 Madchester Rave On

The late Eighties saw a burgeoning music scene in Manchester. This quiz concerns bands, past and present, that hail from that city.

1   Which band had five hit singles in the first three months of 1990?
2   Whose debut album was titled *90*?
3   Which hitmaker started out as a member of that group?
4   Which Manchester band's first live appearance was supporting the Sex Pistols?
5   Who wrote *James Dean Isn't Dead*?
6   Who were the only Mancunian band to hit number one in 1988?
7   Which Mancunian had two American number ones in 1988?
8   Who Broke Out in 1986?
9   Whose first single release was 'Delightful' in 1985?
10 Which band had a hit with their first official single nine years after its release?
11 What is FAC 51, and which band co-owns it?
12 Which large hitmaking conglomerate hail from Old Trafford?
13 Who were In Love With The Girl On A Certain Manchester Megastore Checkout Desk?
14 Which band started life as the Frantic Elevators?
15 Who started out as lead singer of Sixties band Vinegar Joe?
16 Which successful Manchester band were produced by Mickie Most in the Sixties?
17 Which Manchester band were signed by Jonathan King in 1970?
18 Collectively, who are Thomas, Graham, Martyn, Clint and Craig?
19 With which band are Yootha Joyce, Pat Phoenix and Viv Nicholson associated, and why?
20 Which band is led by Mark E. Smith?

28 Green Onions

Are you ecologically aware? How green is your music? This quiz will sort out the Friends Of The Earth from the Plastic People.

A

1 Who hit the Top Ten in 1980 with 'The Earth Dies Screaming'?
2 Who took 'Use It Up And Wear It Out' to number one in 1980?
3 With which band is Green the lead singer?
4 Who took 'Green Door' to number one in 1981?
5 Who topped the charts with 'Green Green Grass Of Home' in 1966?
6 And who went to number one with 'Whispering Grass' in 1975?
7 Who took 'The Air That I Breathe' to number two in 1974?
8 'Flowers In The Rain' was the first record ever played on Radio 1. Who recorded it?
9 Which rock star took up the cause of the Amazonian Indians in the Eighties and involved himself in many fund-raising efforts to save the rain forests?
10 Who decided, "This ain't no ecological breakdown, this is the road to hell" in 1989?
11 Who took a long playing *Journey Through The Secret Life Of Plants*?
12 Who sang that 'Heaven Is A Place On Earth'?
13 What was the name of Alice Cooper's 1989 hit album?
14 Who planted the ' "A" Bomb In Wardour Street' in 1978?
15 What is the title of Terry Wogan's first and only hit single?
16 Who is the only man besides Dave Stewart to have shared a chart duet with Annie Lennox?
17 Who was 'Crushed By The Wheels Of Industry' in 1983?
18 Who hit with 'Now That We've Found Love' in 1978 and 1985?
19 Who sang of 'Doomsday' eight years before she hit the Top Ten with 'High Energy' in 1984?
20 Whose 'Combine Harvester' reaped a rich reward in 1976?

B

1 Who invented the seed drill, died in 1741 and hit number one on the album charts on 6 September 1969?
2 Who advised us to 'Gather In The Mushrooms' in 1961?
3 Who had the biggest hit single with a song called 'Edelweiss'?
4 With which Sixties chart-topping group did Karl Green play guitar?
5 Whose first hit single was called 'Welcome To The Jungle'?
6 Who was the original lead guitarist of Fleetwood Mac?
7 And what was their 'green' hit?
8 Who sang about 'Me And The Farmer' in 1987?
9 Who hit the Top Forty with 'We Kill The World (Don't Kill The World)' in 1981?
10 In the same year, who sang of 'The Elephant's Graveyard (Guilty)'?
11 Which chart-topping band of the Sixties followed up their number

one with 'Green River'?

12 Who pleaded, 'Don't Kill The Whale' in 1978?

13 Whose version of Bob Dylan's 'A Hard Rain's Gonna Fall' hit the Top Ten in 1973?

14 Whose widely played single 'On The Greener Side' surprisingly failed to chart in late 1989?

15 Whose *Village Green Preservation Society* album, though widely praised, also failed to chart in 1968?

16 But which megastar did chart with the single 'Clean Up Your Own Back Yard' in 1969?

17 Which chart-topping band first charted with 'How Will The Wolf Survive' in 1985?

18 Whose single 'Rain Forest' was a hit in both 1984 and 1985?

19 Who sang of 'The Day The World Turned Day-Glo' in 1978?

20 And who celebrated 'The Day The Rains Came' at number one in 1959?

1 Whose first chart LP was called *Get Out And Walk*?

2 Who originally decided in song that "it's not easy being green"?

3 Who sang of 'The Plastic Age' in 1980?

4 Whose 'Plastic Fantastic Lover' was on the B-side of 'White Rabbit'?

5 Whose first hit single in Britain was 'This Planet's On Fire'?

6 Who was digging his (tinned) potatoes in 1965?

7 From which musical does the Clint Eastwood hit 'I Talk To The Trees' come?

8 And from which musical does the song 'Gonna Build A Mountain' come?

9 Who sang, "Someone's dropped a bomb somewhere, contaminating atmosphere and blackening the sky"?

10 And who wrote those lyrics?

11 Whose 1965 hit told us "over and over again, my friend, you don't believe we're on the Eve Of Destruction"?

12 What very ecologically impure song was both the title track of a Rod Stewart album and a hit single for Elkie Brooks?

13 Who wrote the Nashville Teens' hit, 'Tobacco Road'?

14 Whose first British hit single was 'Mannish Boy', five years after his death?

15 Under what group name did John Lydon and Afrika Bambaataa release the single 'World Destruction' in 1985?

16 Whose only album was entitled *Strive To Survive Causing Least Suffering Possible*?

17 Name two of the three acts who hit with 'Green Door' in 1956.

18 Which act scored with an album entitled *End Of Millennium Psychosis Blues* in 1988?

19 Which American country/folk singer charted with 'English Country Garden' in 1962?

20 Which writer about cricket (among other things) played saxophone in Lord Rockingham's XI, who hit number one with 'Hoots Mon' in 1958?

29 Leave Me Alone

In this quiz, we present you with three lists of 31 words. In each list there are 15 pairs and one word which does not pair. So for example there might be *Paul* and *McCartney* among the words in one list, and they would match up. All you have to do is to identify the odd word out in each column, which will then leave you with a three-word name or song title, which is the ultimate answer to this quiz.

	A	**B**	**C**
1	Simon	Duran	Heads
2	Minogue	Luke	Jive
3	Simple	Then	John
4	John	Box	Holly
5	Michael	Ferry	Collins
6	Soft	Michael	Spandau
7	Mel	Matt	Kelly
8	Roses	Band	O'Connor
9	Julian	Red	Stewart
10	Lennon	Black	Marie
11	Ono	Blue	Donny
12	Renato	Jackson	Richard
13	Kim	Five	Johnson
14	Mode	Duran	Ants
15	Houston	Aid	Band
16	George	McDonald	Sinead
17	Garfunkel	Goss	Jon
18	Cafe	George	Dave
19	Melle	Boys	Don
20	Kylie	Janet	Bunny
21	Guns	Sisters	Phil
22	Bowie	Bryan	Cliff
23	Wilde	Bianco	Elton
24	Cell	Simply	Vangelis
25	Depeche	Boy	Buddy
26	Minds	Star	Osmond
27	David	Pointer	Talking
28	Cope	Plastic	Ballet
29	Whitney	Deacon	Chas
30	Sad	Jerico	Adam
31	Renee	London	Rod

30 Sing Our Own Song

Many producers or instrumental groups are no longer prepared to sit back whilst the vocalist grabs the limelight. These days some give only the smallest credit to the singer. This quiz concerns itself with these artists.

A

Who vocalized on the following hits?

1 'Back To Life (However Do You Want Me)'
2 'Pump Up The Jam'
3 'We Call It Acieeed'
4 'Musical Freedom (Movin' On Up)'
5 'Who Found Who'
6 'Paranoimia'
7 'Burn It Up'
8 'Doctorin' The House'
9 'Rok Da House'
10 'People Hold On'

On whose hits did the following vocalists appear?

11 Lisa Marie
12 Adele Bertei
13 Junior Reid
14 Nuff Juice
15 Kool Rock Steady
16 Betty Boo
17 Sylvia Tella
18 Lindy Layton
19 Cathy Dennis
20 Maureen

B

Who helped out on the following?:

1 'Something's Gotten Hold Of My Heart' by Marc Almond
2 'Dead Ringer For Love' by Meat Loaf
3 'I'll Be Good To You' by Quincy Jones
4 'U Got The Look' by Prince
5 'Kiss' by Art Of Noise
6 '(Celebrate) The Day After You' by Blow Monkeys
7 'The Message Is Love' by Arthur Baker
8 'Unconditional Love' by Donna Summer
9 'The Rhythm Divine' by Yello
10 'Indestructible' by the Four Tops

On what tracks do the following combinations appear?

11 Pogues featuring Kirsty MacColl

12 UB40 featuring Chrissie Hynde

13 Clannad featuring Bono

14 Communards featuring Sarah-Jane Morris

15 Art Of Noise featuring Duane Eddy

16 Julio Iglesias featuring Stevie Wonder

17 Fat Boys featuring Chubby Checker

18 U2 featuring B. B. King

19 Philip Bailey featuring Phil Collins

20 Mike Sarne featuring Wendy Richard

C

1 Which saxophonist received credit from Mica Paris?

2 Which keyboardist received credit from the Beatles?

3 Which guitarist received credit from Jean-Michel Jarre?

4 Who sang "I want my MTV" on Dire Straits' 'Money For Nothing'?

5 Who sang "Chaka Khan let me rock you, let me rock you Chaka Khan" on Chaka Khan's 'I Feel For You'?

6 Who sang "Jeux sans frontières" on Peter Gabriel's 'Games Without Frontiers'?

7 Ya Kid K has appeared on hits for which two acts (to mid-1990)?

8 Carol Kenyon appeared on hits for which two acts (to mid-1990)?

9 Merlin has appeared on hits for which two acts (to mid-1990)?

10 Which group appears on 'Song To The Siren' by This Mortal Coil?

11 Which group appears on 'Naughty Girls' by Sam Fox?

12 Which group appears on 'Wipeout' by Fat Boys?

13 Who has received billing from both Radio Heart and Paul Gardiner?

14 Who has received billing from both Michael Jackson and Dennis Edwards?

15 Who has received billing from both Living In A Box and Wilton Felder?

16 What is the connection between Rose Windross and Do'reen?

17 What is the connection between Randy Crawford and Joe Cocker?

18 What is the connection between Einstein and Lonnie Gordon?

19 Richard Darbyshire featured on 'Coming Back For More' for Jellybean. Can you name the group he fronts?

20 Eric and Billy featured on 'Hey Music Lover' for S Express. Can you name the groups that they went on to lead?

31 Laugh At Me

Do you remember all the hits that have tried to make you laugh, and the comedians who sang the tear-jerking hits? If so, you will do well on this quiz. If not, try these out on one of your funnier friends.

A

1   Who teamed up with La Na Nee Nee Noo Noo to take their Comic Relief version of the Beatles' 'Help!' to the Top Three in 1989?

2   What was the title of Spitting Image's 1986 number one?

3   Who put 'Star Trekkin'' at the top of the charts?

4   What was Joe Dolce's only hit, a number one in 1981?

5   What was Benny Hill's only number one?

6   Who were 'Rocking Around The Christmas Tree' in 1987?

7   Who were the most successful comedy recording group of all, with 13 hits including five Top Ten hits over 19 years?

8   Who sang with the Young Ones on their 1986 version of 'Living Doll'?

9   Which Young One reached number two with his remake of Traffic's 'Hole In My Shoe'?

10   Which funnyman had a tragic number one with 'Tears'?

11   Which funnyman had another unfunny chart-topper with 'I Pretend'?

12   Who is the only ventriloquist to have had a Top Ten hit?

13   Which Aussie asked us to 'Tie Me Kangaroo Down Sport'?

14   Whose third number one was called 'My Old Man's A Dustman'?

15   Who hit number one with 'Lily The Pink' in 1968 and 1969?

16   Whose younger brother is Mike McGear, who was part of the 'Lily The Pink' recording group?

17   Which of his many hits did David Bowie record first, although it did not hit the charts until 1973?

18   Who rearranged Tammy Wynette's 'D.I.V.O.R.C.E.' for a 1975 number one?

19   Whose hits include 'Gertcha' and 'Rabbit'?

20   Whose 'Loadsamoney (Doin' Up The House)' hit number four in 1988?

B

1   Which group consists of Bill Oddie, Tim Brooke-Taylor and Graeme Garden?

2   Who hit as the Commentators with 'N-N-Nineteen Not Out'?

3   Who was 'The Oldest Swinger In Town'?

4   Who drove his 'Funky Moped' into the Top Five in 1975?

5   Which comic actor hit with 'Hole In The Ground' and 'Right Said Fred'?

6   Who created 'Snot Rap', all in the best possible taste?

7   Whose second album, released in 1988, was called *Comedy*?

8 Which disc holds the record (to the end of 1989) for the biggest leap to number one, from number 33 to the very top in July 1982?

9 What was the title of Clive Dunn's chart-topping single?

10 Who was 'Rat Rapping' in 1983?

11 Which group took 'Stutter Rap (No Sleep 'Til Bedtime)' to number four at the end of 1987?

12 On which single, a posthumous hit in 1982, does Elvis Presley forget the words and giggle feebly instead?

13 Who combined with Mike Sarne on his 1962 hit 'Will I What'?

14 What was the number one hit by characters from TV's *It Ain't Half Hot Mum*?

15 Whose first hit was 'A Day In The Life Of Vince Prince'?

16 Whose hits included 'El Vino Collapso', 'Superman' and 'Agadoo'?

17 Under what name did Spike Milligan, Peter Sellers and Harry Secombe enjoy two Top Ten hits?

18 Who hit number one with 'The Streak' in 1974?

19 Who performed on the double-sided Christmas 1986 chart single, 'Je T'Aime (Allo Allo)/Rene DMC (Devastating Macho Charisma)'?

20 Who were Alvin, Simon and Theodore, who hit number one in America at Christmas 1958?

1 Whose *We All Had Doctors' Papers* was the first comedy LP to top the charts?

2 Who were Laurie Lingo and the Dipsticks, who hit with 'Convoy G.B.'?

3 What do they have in common with the Pee Bee Squad, 1985 hitmakers with 'Rugged And Mean, Butch And On Screen'?

4 Which comedian hit in 1961 with 'Don't Jump Off The Roof Dad'?

5 And whose only chart attack was the 1985 single, 'Again'?

6 Who was the man behind the Piglets' hit, 'Johnny Reggae'?

7 Who broke into the charts in a small way with 'Splish Splash', 'Mr Custer' and 'My Boomerang Won't Come Back'?

8 Which TV comedy signature tune took Michael Medwin, Bernard Bresslaw, Alfie Bass and Leslie Fyson into the Top Ten in 1958?

9 Which of that quartet hit later that year with 'Mad Passionate Love'?

10 What was Pat Boone's only novelty hit, a number two smash in 1962?

11 Who charted with 'Halfway Down The Stairs' in 1977?

12 Who was the Brat, who served up a 1982 Top Twenty hit, 'Chalk Dust – The Umpire Strikes Back'?

13 Who rewrote Melanie's 'Brand New Key' for a number one in 1976?

14 Which number one did Hylda Baker and Arthur Mullard cover in 1978?

15 What was Laurel and Hardy's number two hit in 1975?

16 Give the line-up of the Four Bucketeers, whose 'Bucket Of Water Song' made such a dent in the charts in 1980.

17 Who were Brown Sauce, 'I Wanna Be A Winner' hitmakers in 1981?

18 What First World War saga was a Top Ten hit for the Royal Guardsmen and the Hotshots?

19 Who did they come to take away ha-haaa in 1966?

20 What song was Shirley Bassey singing as Morecambe and Wise changed her shoes for her in their classic Christmas TV show?

32 Year Of Decision

Quite simply, in which year were these titles at number one?

A

1 'Sealed With A Kiss', 'Ferry 'Cross The Mersey' and 'Something's Gotten Hold Of My Heart'

2 'The Power Of Love', 'Hello' and 'I Just Called To Say I Love You'

3 'You Can't Hurry Love', 'Red Red Wine' and 'Only You'

4 'Stand By Me', 'Everything I Own' and 'Let It Be'

5 'Living Doll', 'Spirit In The Sky' and 'Caravan Of Love'

6 'Imagine', 'One Day In Your Life' and 'Green Door'

7 'I Think We're Alone Now', 'With A Little Help From My Friends' and 'He Ain't Heavy He's My Brother'

8 'Crying', 'Working My Way Back To You' and 'Woman In Love'

9 'I Got You Babe', 'Dancing In The Street' and 'You'll Never Walk Alone'

10 'Happy Talk', 'Save Your Love' and 'Seven Tears'

B

1 'Everything I Own', 'Lonely This Christmas' and 'Annie's Song'

2 'Merry Xmas Everybody', 'Tie A Yellow Ribbon Round The Old Oak Tree' and 'Blockbuster'

3 'Grandad', 'Chirpy Chirpy Cheep Cheep' and 'Ernie (The Fastest Milkman In The West)'

4 'Forever And Ever', 'Mississippi' and 'No Charge'

5 'My Ding-A-Ling', 'Mama Weer All Crazee Now' and 'Long Haired Lover From Liverpool'

6 'Mary's Boy Child', 'Figaro' and 'Dreadlock Holiday'

7 'Stand By Your Man', 'Ms Grace' and 'Hold Me Close'

8 'One Day At A Time', 'Hit Me With Your Rhythm Stick' and 'Ring My Bell'

9 'Show You The Way To Go', 'Float On' and 'Free'

10 'Bridge Over Troubled Water', 'Woodstock' and 'I Hear You Knockin''

C

1 'Day Tripper', 'Ticket To Ride' and 'Help!'

2 'Ob-La-Di Ob-La-Da', 'Two Little Boys' and 'Sugar Sugar'

3 'Telstar', 'Wonderful Land' and 'Nut Rocker'

4 'All You Need Is Love', 'San Francisco (Be Sure To Wear Some Flowers In Your Hair)' and 'A Whiter Shade Of Pale'

5 'Oh Pretty Woman', 'Juliet' and 'Diane'

6   'Little Sister', 'Are You Lonesome Tonight' and 'Surrender'
7   'Diamonds', 'Foot Tapper' and 'Dance On'
8   'These Boots Are Made For Walkin'', 'Strangers In The Night' and 'Distant Drums'
9   'Lily The Pink', 'I Pretend' and 'The Good The Bad And The Ugly'
10   'Starry Eyed', Shakin' All Over' and 'Three Steps To Heaven'

33 Panic

We hope this puzzle does not send you into a panic. It is another acrostic. When filled in with the correct letters, the boxed area quotes the lyric of a well-known song by the same group that had a hit with the single 'Panic'. The letter in the top left corner of each square refers you to the lettered clues. Fill in the clues in the boxes indicated by the numbers. When completed the first letters of clues A through to U spell out the title of the quoted song. AA is an additional clue.

A   Record company founded by Elton John 57 133 36 99 110 11

B   She had a number one with 'Orinoco Flow' 18 103 28 98

C   '83 6 89 97 141 Rooms', Gary Moore hit

D   21 1 129 39 93 Thomas, US soul singer

E   Hit single by group who recorded quoted song 140 78 34

F   62 32 79 12 85 136 Gift, vocalist of Fine Young Cannibals

G   125 70 108 31 51, 128 Wall, album by Michael Jackson (2 words)

H   134 3 48 For Africa, 1985 charity group

I   '73 14 59 22 44 71 64 Tonight', hit by INXS (2 words)

J   '56 10 66 29 40 54 43 23 De Da Da Da', Police single (4 words)

K   '102 126 4 117 38 Frutti', Little Richard classic

L   '123 35 25 90', as Manfred Mann's clown said (2 words)

M   Its headquarters are in Manchester Square, London: 7 47 114

N   'I Will 24 143 13 95 84 120 37 101 53', Little Peggy March 1963 US number one (2 words)

O   Crazy 104 122 86 20, pianist who went to number one in America in 1955 with his eponymous album

P   '116 81 138 68 16 Ladder To The Roof', post-Ross Supremes hit (2 words)

Q   '77 45 2 52 113 100 109 33 Cry' by Sisters of Mercy (3 words)

R   74 9 92 65 White Duke, Bowie persona

S   75 42 49 124, Christian name of bass player in quoted group

T   'Last Of The Famous 5 137 19 50 17 142 41 8 94 26 112 80 135 Playboys', solo hit by lead singer of quoted group

U   115 111 27 Order, act from same city as quoted group

V   '15 131 60 130 63 105', Joan Armatrading favourite

W   67 46 91 30, item worn by clergyman mentioned on the B-side of the title of this quiz

X   132 76 96 55 121 118 139, Little and DeVille

Y   119 127 107 82, dance immortalized by Bobby Freeman

Z 87 72 58 and Cry, duo who broke in 1987

AA What your agent will solve this puzzle for: 61 106 88 69 (2 words)

D	Q	H
1	2	3

K	T	C	M
4	5	6	7

T	R	J
8	9	10

A	F	N	I
11	12	13	14

V	P	T	B
15	16	17	18

T	O	D	I
19	20	21	22

J	N
23	24

L	T	U
25	26	27

B	J	W
28	29	30

G	F	Q	E
31	32	33	34

L
35

A	N	K	D	J
36	37	38	39	40

T	S	J
41	42	43

I	Q	W
44	45	46

M	H	S	T
47	48	49	50

G	Q	N
51	52	53

J	X	J
54	55	56

A	Z	I	V
57	58	59	60

AA	F	V	I	R	J
61	62	63	64	65	66

W	P	AA
67	68	69

G	I	Z	I	R	S	X	Q
70	71	72	73	74	75	76	77

E	F	T	P
78	79	80	81

Y	C
82	83

N	F
84	85

O	Z	AA
86	87	88

C	L	W	R	D
89	90	91	92	93

T	N	X
94	95	96

C	B	A	Q
97	98	99	100

N	K
101	102

B	O	V
103	104	105

AA	Y	G	Q	A	U	T
106	107	108	109	110	111	112

Q	M	U	P	K	X	Y
113	114	115	116	117	118	119

N	X	O	L
120	121	122	123

S	G	K
124	125	126

Y	G	D	V
127	128	129	130

V
131

X	A	H	T	F	T	P
132	133	134	135	136	137	138

X	E	C
139	140	141

T	N
142	143

34 Little Things Mean A Lot

This is the quiz for little people. There have been many songs about little things, many little singers and little albums. These questions test your knowledge about the little things in life.

A

1 Who wanted to be given 'A Little Respect' in 1988?

2 Who took 'Every Little Thing She Does Is Magic' to number one in 1981?

3 Who saw his 'Little Red Corvette' reach number two in 1985?

4 'With A Little Help From My Friends' brought Wet Wet Wet their first number one, but who benefited financially from its success?

5 Who won the Eurovision Song Contest in 1982 with 'A Little Peace'?

6 Who released 'Little Lady' as the follow-up to her number one smash 'Japanese Boy' in 1981?

7 'Mary Had A Little Lamb' and 'With A Little Luck' were Top Ten hits for which McCartney group?

8 Who did the Everly Brothers tell to wake up in 1957?

9 Which British female vocalist, recently connected with the Pet Shop Boys, had a Top Twenty hit with 'Little By Little' in 1966?

10 Which American singer, who enjoyed chart success with New Edition, had a Top Ten hit with 'Every Little Step' in 1989?

11 'Good Golly Miss Molly' brought who a Top Ten hit?

12 Who wanted to be told 'Little Lies' in 1987?

13 Whose *A Little Bit Of This And A Little Bit Of That* album includes the hits 'Put Your Hands Together' and 'C'mon And Get My Love'?

14 What did Olivia Newton-John want a little more of in 1978?

15 Who told us to do 'The Locomotion' in 1962?

16 'Little Red Rooster' brought which UK group their second number one?

17 Who 'Spread A Little Happiness' in 1982?

18 Whose 'Strange Little Girl' gave them their fifth Top Ten hit in 1982?

19 Who took a break from Fleetwood Mac in 1985 to record her *Rock A Little* album?

20 From which Wet Wet Wet album does the Top Ten hit 'Sweet Little Mystery' come?

B

1 Who did David Bowie duet with on 'Peace On Earth – Little Drummer Boy'?

2 Whose 'A Little Bit Of Snow' crept to number 70 in 1987, a far cry from the Top Ten positions which his 'New Song' and 'Look Mama' reached earlier in the Eighties?

3 'Three Little Birds' was a Top Twenty hit for which reggae vocalist?

4 Who sang about 'A Little Boogie Woogie (In The Back Of My Mind)' in 1987?

5 Who was 'A Little In Love' in 1981, and saw his 'Little Town' just fail to provide him with his 48th Top Ten hit a year later?

6   Which trio of sisters followed up the success of 'Little Drummer Boy' with 'Little Donkey' in 1960?

7   What was Feargal Sharkey's follow-up to his number one, 'A Good Heart'?

8   What was Queen's first number one in America, a track which stopped at number two in the UK?

9   Which British group followed up their first number one, 'Bye Bye Baby' with another chart-topper, 'Give A Little Love'?

10   Who took 'A Little Bit Me A Little Bit You' to the Top Three in 1967?

11   Which British vocalist, who hit the top in 1959 with 'Only Sixteen', had another Top Ten smash in 1962 with 'When My Little Girl Is Smiling'?

12   'Poor Little Fool' was the first of four Top Ten hits for which American vocalist in 1958?

13   'His Latest Flame' got to number one for Elvis Presley as a double A-sided single with which other song?

14   Which American group had a 1974 hit with 'You Little Trust Maker'?

15   Whose 'Little White Bull' reached number six in 1959?

16   For which female singer did 'With A Little Love' chart briefly in 1990?

17   'Little Town Flirt' was the sixth Top Ten hit for which American singer who died tragically in 1990?

18   Whose 'Little Willy' reached number four in 1972?

19   'As Tears Go By', 'Come And Stay With Me' and 'This Little Bird' were all Top Ten hits in the Sixties for which female vocalist?

20   'A Little Bit Of Soap' and 'Pretty Little Angel Eyes' were Top five hits for which UK group in the Seventies?

---

1   Who "cried just a little bit" in 1983?

2   Which female vocalist featured on Bomb The Bass's version of 'Say A Little Prayer' in 1988?

3   Who sang about 'Little Arrows' in 1968?

4   In which year did Billy J. Kramer and the Dakotas score their second number one with 'Little Children'?

5   'Takes A Little Time' was a Top Twenty hit for which group in 1985?

6   From which country do the Bouncing Czechs, whose record 'I'm A Little Christmas Cracker' spent a week in the charts at number 72, come a) Czechoslovakia, b) UK or c) Australia?

7   Who released 'Little Boy Sad' as his follow-up to 'You're Sixteen' in 1961?

8   In 1976, which British band had their only hit single with 'Little Does She Know'?

9   Whose album *Little Creatures* reached the Top Ten in 1985?

10   The Banned, the Troggs and Marty Wilde have all tried their luck with songs called 'Little Girl', but who had the biggest hit with that title?

11   Who "told every little star" in 1961?

12   They failed ever to make the single chart in Britain, but found more
     success in the albums chart, where *Time Loves A Hero* reached
     number eight. Name the group.

13   Who had his second Top Ten hit in 1965 with 'Little Things'?

14   From whose *The End Of Innocence* album does the track 'Little Tin
     God' come?

15   Which American group recorded the original version of 'Tears On
     My Pillow', which gave Kylie Minogue her third number one in 1990?

16   What did Mark Wynter ask the little girl to do in 1962?

17   Who were 'Just A Little Bit Too Late' in 1965, a) Wayne Fontana
     and the Mindbenders b) The Rolling Stones or c) Jan and Dean?

18   Of which band was John Farnham a member before his worldwide
     solo chart success with 'You're The Voice'?

19   Which British artist spent his first weeks on the Eighties charts with
     'Little Jeannie'?

20   Who did the Curls help reach the charts for the first time with
     'Seven Little Girls Sitting In The Back Seat'?

---

35 The Big One

**The charts have always been full of songs telling the world how
big our love is, how big the noise is, and in which parts of the
world we are big. Let's see if you can remember who the big stars
are:**

---

1   Which Scottish group, headed by Stuart Adamson, had a string of
     Top Ten hits in the Eighties?

2   'Chantilly Lace' was the only hit for which late American star?

3   Who was having a 'Big Time' in 1987?

4   Who said 'Blame It On The Boogie' in 1989, echoing the Jacksons in
     1978?

5   Who were 'Big In Japan' in 1984?

6   Who first hit the chart with '$E=mc^2$' in 1986?

7   Whose *Big Thing* album included the hits 'I Don't Want Your Love'
     and 'All She Wants Is'?

8   Who had a 'Big Hunk O' Love' in the Top Ten in 1959?

9   Who, according to the Four Seasons, don't cry?

10   Who were looking for 'Big Love' in 1987?

11   Which Tears For Fears album spent 80 weeks on the charts in the
     Eighties?

12   Whose first greatest hits album was called *Big Hits (High Tide And
     Green Grass)*?

13   Who had a Top Ten album called *Big Bang* in 1989?

14   What was Jimmy Dean's 1961 smash hit about a bad coal miner?

15   What title was used for different Top Twenty smashes in the
     Eighties by Kool And The Gang, the Gap Band and Inner City?

16 Which Kate Bush album contained the 1986 hit, 'The Big Sky'?

17 Name Wham's second album.

18 What was the Smiths' follow-up to 'The Boy With The Thorn In His Side'?

19 Who did Haysi Fantayzee describe as big leggy?

20 Who are possibly big, and had a birdhouse in their soul in 1990?

B

1 Who sang about life in the 'Big Apple' in 1983?

2 Whose 'Big Log' just missed the Top Ten, also in 1983?

3 Whose 'Sideshow' raced to number three in 1976?

4 Who claimed to be 'Big In America' in 1986?

5 Who said, in 1974, 'This Town Ain't Big Enough For Both Of Us'?

6 Who hit with their version of Bruce Springsteen's 'Dancing In The Dark' in 1985?

7 Who was responsible for 'Big Six', 'Big Seven', 'Big Eight' and 'Big Ten'?

8 And on the same theme, what name did Doc Cox use to record 'The Winker's Song (Misprint)'?

9 Who lived and recorded at Big Pink in Woodstock, New York, in the late Sixties?

10 What was the main title of the Style Council's 1984 hit which was subtitled '(You're The Best Thing/Big Boss Groove)'?

11 Who complained that "a big yellow taxi came and took away my old man"?

12 Which song, recorded but not written by the Beatles, included the line, "they're gonna make a big star out of me"?

13 Who first hit with 'Proud Mary', whose "big wheel keeps on turning"?

14 Who hit the Top Twenty with 'The Big Beat' in 1958?

15 What was Then Jerico's first Top Ten hit album called?

16 Who were John Gustavson, Brian Griffiths and Johnny Hutchinson?

17 And who were Cass Elliott, Tim Rose and Jim Hendricks?

18 What was Cliff Richard's next Top Ten hit after 'Congratulations'?

19 Who took 'Big Man' to number two in 1958?

20 Whose hits included 'I (Who Have Nothing)', 'Something' and 'Big Spender'?

C

1 Who helped Simon Dupree fly his 'Kites' in the Top Ten in 1967?

2 Which Banjo Band got together to reach the Top Ten in 1954?

3 With which San Francisco band did Janis Joplin first hit the US charts?

4 What was the title of the first chart single by That Petrol Emotion?

5 Whose three hits which did *not* hit the Top Ten were called 'Sunny Day', 'Getting Up' and 'The Big Bean'?

6 Who took 'A Fifth Of Beethoven' to number one in America in 1976?

7 What title was used by Jean Knight for a US number two hit in 1971, and by Heavy D. and the Boyz to hit number 61 in Britain in 1986?

8 What was Zoot Money's backing group called?

9 And what was their only hit single?

10 Who are Simon Tedd and Shark, who first hit the charts in 1989?

11 By what name is American rapper Antonio Hardy better known?

12 And who are Julie Hadwen, Tony Burke, Steve Martinez and Mace?

13 Who hit with 'Don't Walk' and 'Please Yourself' in 1986 and 1987?

14 'Big Boss Man' was an American hit in 1967, but not in the UK. For whom?

15 One week at number 30, the lowest chart rank on 12 February 1960, was Toni Fisher's entire British chart career. What was her hit?

16 Two different acts hit in 1977 and 1989. The first act hit number four with 'Romeo' and the second managed one week on the album charts with its eponymous debut set. What name do they share?

17 Which transatlantic chart-topper had a US hit with 'Big Shot' in 1979?

18 Which transatlantic chart-toppers had a US hit with 'Big Man In Town' in 1964?

19 Whose first and last hit was an LP called *The Swimmer* in 1986?

20 Which band, whose name means "big" in Russian, had one week on the albums chart at number 100 with its only hit, *Lindy's Party*, in 1987?

---

36 I'd Rather Jack

This quiz is about the most successful production/songwriting team in recent years – Stock Aitken Waterman.

1 What are the respective Christian names of the three producers?

2 Under what pseudonym did Waterman hit the charts in 1975?

3 And what was the song?

4 Before teaming up with Waterman, Stock and Aitken released a Frankie Goes To Hollywood parody – what was it called?

5 What was the trio's first hit as a production team?

6 And their first number one?

7 What does PWL stand for?

8 SAW had the biggest selling single of 1987 – what was it?

9 What is the biggest selling SAW production (to mid-1990)?

10 Why did Waterman take out a court injunction against M/A/R/R/S?

11 What character did Jason Donovan play in *Neighbours*?

12 Kylie and Jason have both hit number one with cover versions – name the songs and the artists that had the original hits.

13 Apart from the multi-million selling Kylie and Jason albums, the PWL label released only one other album in the Eighties – what was it?

14 What was Kylie's follow-up to 'The Loco-Motion' in America?

15 To mid-1990, which three charity number ones have SAW produced?

16 With which French soloist did the team have a minor hit?

17 What is Sonia's surname?

18 Which two 'Supreme' artists have benefited from the sound of SAW?

19 The SAW track 'Mr Sleaze' was the B-side to which Top Ten hit?

20 SAW have produced Top Ten hits for two artists who had already long established careers – who?

21 Which two Capital Radio DJs have SAW produced hits for?

22 In aid of which charity?

23 Name Brother Beyond's two SAW produced hits.

24 Collectively, who are Jason John, Phil Creswick and Mark Gillespie?

25 Name five SAW productions with 'Heart' in the title.

 # Starman

Space travel has always fascinated pop music makers, as this quiz shows. Every question has some connection, however vague, with the planets, the stars and space. Let's start with the easy ones:

A

1   Which Pink Floyd album spent almost 300 weeks on the charts?

2   What was David Bowie's first number one?

3   In which other number one did Bowie admit "Major Tom's a junkie"?

4   Which Jeff Wayne track did Ben Liebrand remix into the Top Three of the singles charts at the end of 1989?

5   And from what album was it taken?

6   Whose first hit was 'Love Missile F1-11' in 1986?

7   Which planet did Don Pablo's Animals take to the Top Ten in 1990?

8   What was Chris De Burgh's Christmas hit 1986?

9   Who recorded 'Telstar', a number one hit in 1962?

10 Whose 'Clouds Across The Moon' interrupted an intergalactic phone call in 1985?

11 Where did Ziggy Stardust's spiders come from?

12 Which two planets featured in the title of Wings' number one album from 1975?

13 Where were the Police walking at number one in December 1979?

14 Who is the lead singer of Queen?

15 Who was "Star Trekkin' across the universe" in 1987?

16 Whose first hit single was 'Planet Earth'?

17 Who hit number one by 'Doctorin' The Tardis'?

18 Who came back 'Down To Earth' in 1986?

19 What was Elton John's second hit?

20 On which planet did David Bowie want to know if there was life?

B

1 Which Carpenters' hit was subtitled '(The Recognized Anthem Of World Contact Day)'?
2 Who had Top Ten albums with *Journey To The Centre Of The Earth* and *No Earthly Connection*?
3 Whose only hit was 'Magic Fly', a number two hit in 1977?
4 Which reggae artist hit with 'Dat' and 'Your Honour'?
5 And which band climbed to number 22 in 1987 with 'Satellite'?
6 What was Peter Schilling's Bowie-based 1984 hit single?
7 Which group hit the Top Ten in 1974 and 1975 with 'Rocket' and 'Moonshine Sally'?
8 Whose first album, a Top Twenty hit in 1988, was entitled *Just Visiting This Planet*?
9 Who had a hit album that same year, called *Aliens Ate My Buick*?
10 Who had the Top Twenty hit with the theme from *E.T.*?
11 What was Earth Wind And Fire's planetary hit in 1978?
12 Which band claimed 'I'm The Urban Spaceman'?
13 Which spaceship did Adam Ant ride into the Top Twenty in 1984?
14 Who had the original hit with the song mentioned in question 7 of Section A?
15 Which band hit number 34 with 'Space Age Love Song' in 1982?
16 Which film theme, by Meco, hit number one in the USA and number seven in UK in 1977?
17 Which number one single came from an album titled *The Stars We Are*?
18 Who said *Aloha From Hawaii Via Satellite* in 1973?
19 Whose 1989 debut album was entitled *Shooting Rubber Bands At The Stars*?
20 Who admitted, 'I Lost My Heart To A Starship Trooper' in 1978, but married somebody even richer?

C

1 What was the title of the B52s' album from which 'Love Shack' was taken?
2 What American number one hit was covered by Dickie Valentine in 1959, and re-entered the charts four times?
3 Which planet was in blue jeans for Mark Wynter in 1962?
4 Which Swedish instrumental group hit with 'Rocket Man' in 1962?
5 And which Dutch duo took 'Woodpeckers From Space' to number 72 for one week in October 1985?
6 Whose only hit was 'Can't Stop Running', a number 53 hit in 1983?
7 What was the Rezillos' interplanetary destination in 1978?
8 Who fancied 'Breakfast On Pluto' in 1969?
9 What number space station did both Sammy Hagar and Montrose turn into a hit?
10 Who played the 'Space Bass' in 1979?
11 What was Afrika Bambaataa's first chart outing in Britain?
12 What was the name of Sheb Wooley's one-eyed, one-horned alien?

13 What song was a hit for both Ella Fitzgerald and Gloria Gaynor, but is more usually associated with Les Paul and Mary Ford?

14 Which Cliff Richard hit of the Fifties had lyrics about "sailing 'cross the stars up to a silvery moon"?

15 Who took 'Outta Space' to number two in the USA, and number 44 here?

16 Vangelis hit the Top Fifty in 1981 with 'Heaven And Hell, Third Movement'. For which TV series was this the theme?

17 Which Fifties drummer led The Rockets?

18 Which Jamaican singer had one week of chart fame in 1970 with 'Moon Hop'?

19 Who recorded the instrumental 'Stars Fell On Stockton'?

20 Which number one hitmaker offered to pay to go into space as a passenger on a Russian space flight?

38 Si Si Je Suis Un Rock Star

How good are you on EuroPop? Do you have Swahili A-Level? How many foreign language hits over the years do you remember, and how many foreign hitmakers can you recall?

1 Who hit number one in 1987 with 'La Bamba'?

2 And in what language was it sung?

3 What was Jimmy Somerville's French language hit of 1990?

4 Who brought 'Lambada' to the UK charts at the end of 1989?

5 What was the English title of the number one hit called in Spanish 'Volver A Empezar'?

6 And who took it to number one?

7 Who did Vanessa Paradis introduce to the Top Ten in 1988?

8 What was the title of the Japanese language hit for Kyu Sakamoto?

9 Which Englishwoman and Frenchman combined for a number one with 'Je T'Aime . . . Moi Non Plus' in 1969?

10 Which French vocalist invited us on a 'Voyage Voyage' in 1988?

11 The first foreign language chart-topper was an instrumental movie theme by the Mantovani orchestra. What was it (and the film) called?

12 Which German group made a 'Tour De France' and an 'Autobahn'?

13 In what language did Massiel sing her Eurovision winner 'La La La'?

14 In what language was Izhar Cohen's Eurovision winner 'A Ba Ni Bi'?

15 Cohen's compatriot hit with 'Im Nin'Alu' in 1988. Who was she?

16 'Sie Liebt Dich' and 'Komm, Gib Mir Deine Hand' were German recordings for which group?

17 Which Swedish lady hit with the holiday favourite 'Y Viva España'?

18 Dusty Springfield took 'Io Che No Viva Senza Te' to the top. What was it called in English?

19 Which Edith Piaf song did Grace Jones hit with in 1986?

20 In what language was Nicole's 'A Little Peace' originally sung?

B

1. Who hit the Top Ten with 'Pie Jesu' in 1985?
2. Who hit number 14 at Christmas 1973 with 'Gaudete'?
3. What Latin plainsong, which gave Paul Phoenix a small hit in 1979, was used as the theme of the TV series *Tinker, Tailor, Soldier, Spy*?
4. What was the country of origin of Les Troubadours du Roi Baudouin come, whose single 'Sanctus' was featured in the film *If*?
5. What was the Singing Nun's only hit?
6. Who hit with 'Tous Les Garçons Et Les Filles' in 1964?
7. What was Plastic Bertrand's Top Ten hit in 1978?
8. What was Manhattan Transfer's 1977 number one called?
9. Who recorded the English original of Mirielle Mathieu's hit, 'La Dernière Valse'?
10. Whose original version of 'Milord' in 1960 was a bigger hit than Frankie Vaughan's English language cover?
11. Which 1958 Italian smash hit was unsuccessfully revived by the Gipsy Kings in 1989?
12. What was Sweet People's 1980 Top Five hit called (in French)?
13. On which album did Queen sing in Japanese on 'Te O Toriatte'?
14. On which album did Elvis sing in German on 'Wooden Heart'?
15. On which album did Fairport Convention sing in French on 'Si Tu Dois Partir'?
16. On which album did the Beatles sing in French on 'Michelle'?
17. Which soundtrack album featured Deodato's 'Also Sprach Zarathustra'?
18. In which language was Trio's 'Da Da Da' originally recorded?
19. Which tune, popularized by the Muppets, gave Piero Umiliani a surprise Top Ten hit in 1977?
20. Frenchman Ryan Paris hit the Top Ten in 1983 with an Italian title. What was it?

C

1. In which language was the spoken section of Simon Dupree's 1967 Top Ten hit, 'Kites'?
2. Which 1966 Top Ten hit featured a spoken section which began, "The words mean, I am a truthful man from the land of the palm trees"?
3. Who, apart from George Baker, hit with 'Una Paloma Blanca'?
4. What was the Radha Krishna Temple's unlikely hit of 1969?
5. What was Mory Kante's Top Thirty hit of 1988 called?
6. What song by the Pop Tops was covered in English by Roger Whittaker, giving both acts Top Forty hits in 1971?
7. What song was a hit in 1960 for both the Egyptian Bob Azzam and the French Staiffi and his Mustafas?
8. What was coupled with Siouxsie & the Banshees' 1982 hit 'Melt'?
9. What was Bimbo Jet's 1975 Top Twenty hit?
10. Who is Romania's only hitmaker, who piped his way into the Top Ten in 1976 with 'Doina De Jale (Light Of Experience)'?
11. Whose late Seventies hits include 'Super Nature' and 'Je Suis Music'?

12 Who was the solo clarinettist on Chris Barber's classic 'Petite Fleur'?

13 With which song did Sweden's Herreys win Eurovision in 1984?

14 The Browns had the English hit version of 'The Three Bells', but who took the original French song into the Top Thirty in 1959?

15 Who took all three late Fifties Italian classics, 'Volare', 'Ciao Ciao Bambina' and 'Come Prima' into the UK charts?

16 The first Eurovision winner to hit our charts was 'Tom Pillibi' by Jacqueline Boyer in 1960. For which country did she win?

17 The first Eurovision winner in a foreign language to hit our Top Ten was 'Un Banc, Un Arbre, Une Rue' in 1971. Who sang it?

18 What was the original version of Nena's '99 Red Balloons' called?

19 What was Gigliola Cinquetti's Eurovision winner called?

20 In what foreign language did Peter MacJunior sing 'The Water Margin'?

Michael Jackson Medley

Like the Lady Madonna quiz, we are asking you to identify various Michael Jackson hits by a snatch of the lyrics. Some of the lyrics come from songs by Michael and other artists, so be careful.

A

1 "A lot of people misunderstand me/That's because they don't know me at all"

2 "People always told me be careful of what you do/And don't go around breaking young girls' hearts"

3 "I think I told you I'm a lover not a fighter"

4 "You'll remember me somehow/Though you don't need me now/I will stay in your heart/And when things fall apart/You'll remember"

5 "With a girl to call my own/I'll never be alone/And you my friend will see you got a friend in me"

6 "We can change the world tomorrow/This could be a better place/If you don't like what I'm saying/Then won't you slap my face"

7 "You hear the door slam/And realise there's nowhere left to run"

8 "You better run you better do what you can/Don't wanna see no blood"

9 "I know your every move/So won't you just let me be/I've been here many times before/But I was too blind to see"

10 "He rocks in the treetops all day long/Hoppin' and a-boppin' and singing his song"

B

1 "I'm melting like hot candle wax"

2 "I've learned that love's not possession/And I've learned that love won't wait"

3 "She's always gone too long/Anytime she goes away/Wonder this time where she's gone"

4 "When you return to your home town/And discuss your trip/Will I be the guy that put you down/Or someone that you don't forget"

5 "Oh baby give me one more chance/Won't you let me back in your heart"

6 "Come on, come on, come on let me show you what it's all about"

7 "We can come together and think like one/Live together underneath the sun"

8 "Out on the floor there ain't nobody like us/But when you dance there's a magic that must be love"

9 "My baby's always dancing/And it wouldn't be a bad thing/But I don't get no loving"

10 "We're all the same yes the blood inside of me is inside of you"

1 "Gotta hide your inhibitions/Gotta let that fool loose deep inside your soul"

2 "I know she loves me 'cause when I look in her eyes, I realise I need her sharing her world beside me"

3 "You're just a product of loveliness/I like the groove of your walk, your talk, your dress"

4 "Let me fill your heart with joy and laughter/Togetherness girl is all I'm after"

5 "Darling look both ways before you cross me/You're heading for a danger zone"

6 "You used to take and deceive me, now who is sorry now"

7 "Billie Jean is always talkin'/When nobody else is talkin'/Tellin' lies and rubbin' shoulders/So they called her mouth a motor"

8 "She ran underneath the table/He could see she was unable/So she ran into the bedroom"

9 "Standing here/Baptised in all my tears/Baby through the years/You know I'm crying"

10 "You're the spark that lit the flame inside of me and you do know that I love it"

40 Nice Legs, Shame About The Face

We have found some pictures of famous and not-so-famous recording stars, but have separated their faces from their legs. You have to match the face with the correct legs, and put a name to the combination. One mark for each feat correctly performed.

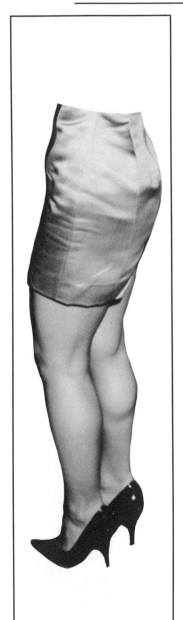

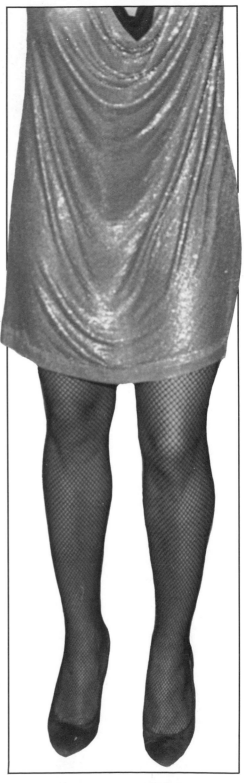

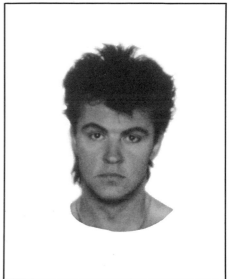

41 Song Sung Blue

Blue can signify happiness, as in "bluebirds over the white cliffs of Dover", or sadness, as in 'Blue Christmas'. Sometimes, when the songwriter is feeling really imaginative, it just means the colour blue. Test whether you've got the blues.

A

Who had hits with the following?

1 'Blue Savannah'
2 'Union City Blue'
3 'Blue Monday'
4 'Forever In Blue Jeans'
5 'I Guess That's Why They Call It The Blues'
6 'Blue Jean'
7 'Visions In Blue'
8 'Bell Bottom Blues'
9 'Blue Peter'
10 'Ocean Blue'
11 'Pale Blue Eyes'
12 'Smuggler's Blues'
13 'Blue Turns To Grey'
14 'Pinky Blue'
15 'Lovesick Blues'
16 'Blue Guitar'
17 'Mean Woman Blues'
18 'Blue Bayou'
19 'Theme From *Hill Street Blues*'
20 'Subterranean Homesick Blues'

B

Who had album hits with the following titles?

1 *True Blue*
2 *Almost Blue*
3 *Dream Of The Blue Turtles*
4 *Red Hot Rhythm 'N' Blues*
5 *G.I. Blues*
6 *Blue Bell Knoll*
7 *Famous Blue Raincoat*
8 *Blues From A Gun*
9 *Gladsome Humour And Blue*
10 *Café Bleu*

The following were all hits by artists with a blue connection, who?

11 'Fergus Sings The Blues'
12 'Blue World'
13 'I Want To Be Your Property'
14 'The Downtown Lights'
15 'Yeh Yeh'
16 'Don't Fear The Reaper'
17 'Last Train To San Fernando'
18 'Melting Pot'
19 'Young At Heart'
20 'Cry Boy Cry'

1   Matt Bianco's Mark Reilly was singer with which group?
2   Which jazz label has been in operation since 1939?
3   Who wrote 'Blue Moon'?
4   'Mr Blue' was an American number one for which act?
5   What were the names of John Belushi and Dan Ackroyd in the movie, *The Blues Brothers*?
6   What is Barry Blue's real name?
7   Who sang "Blue blue electric blue, that's the colour of my room"?
8   Of which group was Lisa Stansfield once a member?
9   Which three 'Blue' football teams have made it to the charts?
10 Whose final hit was 'Angel In Blue'?
11 Which hit was subtitled '(Nel Blu Dipinto Di Blu)'?
12 Which hit song began, "The sun is out, the sky is blue, there's not a cloud to spoil the view"?
13 Which is the odd one out of 'Blue Christmas', 'Blue Suede Shoes', 'Blue River' and 'Blue Guitar'?
14 Which is the odd one out of 'Blue Christmas', 'Blue Moon', 'True Blue' and 'Singing The Blues'?
15 Who had a hit with 'Happy (Love Theme From *Lady Sings The Blues*)'?

42 Food For Thought

Food and drink have been the subject of almost as many songs as love and hate. This quiz finds out whether the way to your musical heart is through your stomach.

A

1 Which double number one hit had the subtitle '(Feed The World)'?
2 Which all-girl band hit the Top Ten with five out of its first six chart entries, the exception being called 'Cheers Then'?
3 Whose debut album was called *Raw Like Sushi*?
4 What was Shakin' Stevens' first hit single called?
5 Where did the guy who swears he's Elvis work, according to Kirsty MacColl?
6 Which band hit number one in 1977 with 'So You Win Again'?
7 Which meaty production duo gave Yazz her first chart break?
8 Which band first hit the top of the charts with 'Going Underground'?
9 And whose first hit album was called *Bat Out Of Hell*?
10 Which spicy female duo had a monster 1988 smash with 'Push It'?
11 What was the title of the Archies' only number one hit single?
12 And what was the name of the song Bobby Goldsboro took twice to number two, in 1968 and 1975?
13 Who took the label credit on hits in the late Eighties featuring vocals by Elisa Fiorillo, Richard Darbyshire and Adele Bertei among others?
14 Who had Eighties hits with 'Cherry Oh Baby' and 'Red Red Wine'?
15 Who said they were 'The King Of Rock 'N' Roll' in 1988?
16 Who hit in the same year with 'Chocolate Girl'?
17 Which Birmingham comic hit the Top Ten on his 'Funky Moped'?
18 What did Toto Coelo eat in 1982?
19 Which sweet-sounding group backed the vocal talents of Phil Fearon?
20 Which chart-toppers are a mixture of champagne and orange juice?

B

1 Who sang "I like bread and butter, I like toast and jam" in 1964?
2 Who topped the charts a year earlier with 'Sweets For My Sweet'?
3 Which film stars hit with the love song 'Bangers And Mash' in 1961?
4 Who asked for 'Two Pints Of Lager And A Packet Of Crisps Please'?
5 What was the only hit for Ohio Express – a tasty dance tune in 1968?
6 In the Fifties, who had a double-sided hit with 'Long Tall Sally' and 'Tutti Frutti'?
7 And in the same decade, which pianist followed up two number ones with 'China Tea'?
8 Who wanted to have 'Dinner With Gershwin' in 1987?
9 Who made a minor impact on the charts in 1984 with his Michael Jackson parody 'Eat It'?

10 What was the name of Marmalade's only chart-topper?

11 Which song was a hit for Harry Belafonte, Shirley Bassey and the Tarriers in 1957?

12 Who guested for 'Breakfast In Bed' with UB40?

13 Which Japanese dish was successful for both Kenny Ball and Kyu Sakamoto in 1963?

14 Which band consisted of Noel Edmonds, John Craven, Maggie Philbin and Keith Chegwin?

15 Who hit number one with the album *Eat To The Beat*?

16 And who hit number two with 'Brown Sugar' in 1971?

17 Where did Supertramp have breakfast in 1979?

18 Who complained about 'The Bitterest Pill (I Ever Had To Swallow)'?

19 Whose only Top Forty hit in nine chart entries was the number eight hit 'Rip It Up' in 1983?

20 And whose only hit was 'The Rain', number four at the end of 1986?

1 Who sang about 'A Pub With No Beer' in 1959?

2 What was the name of Gay Gordon's band, who brushed the charts at Christmas 1986?

3 Whose only concern in 1986 was 'Do Fries Go With That Shake?'

4 Who was the Tornadoes' guitarist who went solo and was soon heard 'Diggin' My Potatoes'?

5 Which group had a 1968 hit with a song which sums up the feelings of all who work with the authors of this book, 'Rice Is Nice'?

6 Who are David Newton, Paul Marsh, Anthony Lineham and Keith Rowley?

7 Who hit with 'Toast' in 1978?

8 'Jambalaya', which has been a hit for both Fats Domino and the Carpenters, mentions crawfish pie and filet gumbo. Which country music superstar wrote it?

9 Who hit in 1984 with 'TV Dinners'?

10 What was Hot Butter's only hit?

11 Which band covered an Abba hit and climbed higher than the Swedes?

12 Who was the lead vocalist on Chas McDevitt's hit, 'Freight Train'?

13 Who starred in the short movie, *Rhythm And Greens*?

14 Who sang about 'Tom's Diner' in 1987?

15 What song links Kim Wilde and Vanilla Fudge?

16 What was the 1910 Fruitgum Co.'s only hit?

17 What was Rodger Collins' only hit?

18 Under what name have Francine Barker, Marlene Mack and Linda Green all recorded?

19 Who had too much to dream last night?

20 Who complained that 'You'll Always Find Me In The Kitchen At Parties'?

43 The Letter

Each clue suggests a cryptic answer. The answer is the title of a hit song by the artist indicated with only one letter removed. The absence of the letter gives the phrase a whole new meaning. For example, if the clue is "Michael Jackson records a commercial', the answer is "Ad", his hit title 'Bad' with one letter ("B") removed.

It is possible, of course, that you might produce a perfectly valid answer different from the one given by the authors. In that case award yourself a bonus point!

A

1 Bros ask Chicken Licken for a career omen
2 The Beatles grant a licence to exterminate
3 Kenny Rogers serenades a young boy
4 The Pretenders have a fish down their trousers
5 Joni Mitchell gets a large Inland Revenue demand on canary paper
6 Kylie Minogue discovers sailors in her bed
7 Prince faces an emergency
8 Led Zeppelin take the steps to sanctuary
9 The B-52s are in a beautiful bag
10 Rod Stewart identifies Carole Thatcher's mother
11 Yes, that figure is 100% Spagna
12 Snap know a debtor
13 Spandau Ballet are aged
14 Elvis Presley faces a ban on his stuffed animal
15 Bill Haley and His Comets dance about the rooster
16 The Hollies know a lightweight nuisance
17 George Michael can hardly bring himself to admit he hasn't got an automobile
18 Lesley Gore doesn't want any other actress getting her role
19 Ben E. King loves to be beside the seashore
20 Soft Cell coloured their affection

B

1 Johnny Logan knows Van Gogh only needed one anyway
2 Whitney Houston reveals who Alfred E. Neuman loves most
3 Shirley Bassey has a divine digit
4 Robin Beck gets aggressive
5 The enemies of Wet Wet Wet prove most useful
6 Donna Summer's eating companion is funny
7 Elton John knows your baby boy
8 Eddie Cochran fools the world
9 Phil Collins recommends speedy romance
10 Louis Armstrong thinks the letters W, H, A and T go together beautifully

11 Roy Orbison has an unhappy transvestite friend
12 Madness enjoy watering the garden
13 The Drifters have female friends in the London Marathon
14 Gerry Rafferty lives on a road of cake makers
15 Freda Payne will not invest in precious metals
16 Madonna doesn't want to hear a sermon of nonsense
17 The Beach Boys criticize a squalid sea craft
18 All Wink Martindale sees are villains
19 J.T. and the Big Family take a holiday in the sun
20 Procol Harum's friend is the only one without a suntan

1 Billy Ocean requests you leave his library and enter his automobile
2 Instead of nightclubbing, the First Edition recommend massage
3 The Rolling Stones ban trespassers on their allotment
4 Cliff Richard covers an ELO hit
5 Chris Rea is listening to the *Well-Tempered Clavier* again
6 Diana Ross's Wall Street investments are looking good
7 Gene Pitney feels nostalgia for one of David Shilling's models
8 The Police's girlfriend is so like the Three Wise Men
9 The stiff breeze causes Peter Paul and Mary to lean forward
10 The Platters honour the man who pays their royalties
11 T'Pau serenade Rodin's *The Thinker*
12 The Bee Gees are bored with the predictable election result
13 The Tams like droopy flesh
14 The Temptations spend all their time in the library
15 The Stargazers can't keep their hairpieces on
16 Barbra Streisand has a romantic Arabian holiday
17 Jimmy Somerville knows the colour of his labia
18 The Smiths don't find millinery as amusing as it used to be
19 Del Shannon has his personal coquette
20 The Communards will not wash like that

44 Calling Your Name

Neither the Smiths nor Bros were particularly imaginative when deciding on their name, although they probably took a little more time than the Nolans to think it up. This quiz focuses on how artists chose their name.

A

Which group was named after:
1 Buddy Holly?
2 The first book of the Bible?
3 A cocktail of champagne and orange juice?
4 An unemployment benefit form?
5 The size and sex of the three members?
6 A set of condiments?
7 Debbie Harry's hair colour?
8 The financial difficulties the group once faced?

Why were the following so named?
9 Abba
10 Bananarama
11 Thompson Twins
12 Fleetwood Mac
13 Jackson Five
14 Ferry Aid
15 Bon Jovi

B

Which group was named after:
1 A character in the TV series *Star Trek*?
2 A disease of sheep and cattle?
3 A newspaper headline about Frank Sinatra?
4 A Bette Davis film?
5 An 18th-century agriculturalist?
6 A Fifties bouffant hairstyle?
7 The Paris commune of 1871?
8 A character in the film *Barbarella*?

In what language are the following names and what is the English translation?
9 Depeche Mode
10 Status Quo
11 Pogues
12 Kraftwerk
13 Scritti Politti
14 Clannad
15 Aswad

Which group was named after:

1 A secondhand furniture store in Hull?

2 A dance style created by Emil-Jacques Dalcrose?

3 A German art movement?

4 An Australian slang word for an asylum?

5 The effects of dexedrine?

The following groups took their monickers from novels. Can you name the book and the author?

6 Heaven 17

7 Tears For Fears

8 Steely Dan

9 Boomtown Rats

10 Level 42

11 Marillion

Why were the following so named?

12 Joy Division

13 M/A/R/R/S

14 Pink Floyd

15 Guns N' Roses

45 Sunshine On Leith

In 1600, Shakespeare had a huge hit with a song with a chorus that went "The rain it raineth every day". A hundred and fifty years later, Dr Johnson (who never managed that elusive hit single) noted that "when two Englishmen meet, their first talk is of the weather". Things have not changed since, but how many of these musical weather forecasts do you remember?

1 Where did the sun always shine for A-Ha?

2 Who hit with 'Wild Is The Wind' and 'When The Wind Blows'?

3 Which weatherman did the Tribe Of Toffs sing an ode to?

4 What did Phil Collins wish it would do, early in 1990?

5 Which rock band had hits with, among others, 'Rain', 'Ice In The Sun' and 'Red Sky'?

6 What song was a hit for Lee Greenwood and Bette Midler?

7 What was the Weather Girls' number two hit in 1984?

8 Who wrote 'Blowin' In The Wind' and 'Rainy Day Women Nos. 12 & 35'?

9 Whose album *Raindancing* hit number two in 1987?

10 Who said she could feel the earth move in 1990?

11 With what band is Phil Bailey the drummer?

12 Who hit number one with 'Give It Up' in 1983?

13 What song title was used by Shakin' Stevens and Darts for (different) hit records?

14 Where was Billy Idol hot in 1982 and, re-mixed, in 1988?

15 Who released the album *Storm Front* in 1989?

16 Who had a 1988 hit with Paul Simon's 'Hazy Shade Of Winter'?

17 Who fronted the heavy metal band Rainbow?

18 What was Terry Jacks' only chart-topper, in 1974?

19 Who were Frankie Valli, Bob Gaudio, Tommy de Vito and Nick Massi?

20 Who was 'Cloudbusting' in 1985?

B

1 Who hit number four with 'Thunder In The Mountains' in 1981?

2 Who wrote Leo Sayer's 1978 chart entry, 'Raining In My Heart'?

3 Who featured the didgeridoo on his Top Three hit, 'Sun Arise'?

4 Who got to number one with 'Something In The Air'?

5 Which chart-topping band began their chart career with 'Chasing For The Breeze' in 1984?

6 Where did Randy Crawford spend a rainy night in 1981?

7 Where did the Artists United Against Apartheid say they would not play in 1985?

8 Who had a number one album with *Fog On The Tyne*?

9 Which band had Seventies Top Ten hits with 'Boogie Nights' and 'Mind Blowing Decisions'?

10 What was the hit song from the film *Butch Cassidy And The Sundance Kid*?

11 Which American trio hit number one with 'The Sun Ain't Gonna Shine Anymore'?

12 Which band hit with 'Walking On Sunshine' in 1985?

13 And what was their only other hit, in 1986?

14 Who hit number four with a different song called 'Walking On Sunshine' in 1982?

15 What song has been a hit single for Bobby Hebb, Cher, Georgie Fame and Boney M?

16 Whose third hit was 'The Wind Cries Mary'?

17 And do you have the foggiest idea what his second hit was?

18 Whose two biggest hits were 'Catch The Wind' and 'Sunshine Superman'?

19 Who hit the Top Twenty in 1987 with 'Let My People Go-Go'?

20 What was Deacon Blue's 1987 hit album called?

C

1 What was Marvin Rainwater's number one hit?

2 And what was Jane Morgan's chart-topper nine months later?

3 Who charted with 'Windpower' in 1982?

4 Which instrumental outfit hit with 'Red River Rock' and 'Rocking Goose'?

5   What was the follow-up to John Leyton's chart-topping 'Johnny Remember Me'?

6   What was the third of Frank Ifield's consecutive number one hits?

7   Who recorded the 1990 hit album 'Flood'?

8   What was Michael Jackson's final Motown Top Ten hit, in 1984?

9   Who got to number one in America with 'Windy', a song which missed out altogether in the UK?

10 What was the B-side of the Beatles' 'Paperback Writer'?

11 What was Spandau Ballet's follow-up to 'To Cut A Long Story Short'?

12 Whose 1989 album was called *Hot In The Shade*?

13 Who had a hit single and album in 1983, both called 'Thunder And Lightning'?

14 What was Enya's 1989 hit single, which only reached number 41?

15 Which Seventies band took their name from the way Eskimos judge the coldness of the Arctic night?

16 Who was the lead vocalist of Amen Corner, who also had hits under his own name and as Fair Weather?

17 Who was 'Snowbound For Christmas' in 1957?

18 From which Sixties film did the instrumental duet 'Foggy Mountain Breakdown' come?

19 What is the surname of American hitmakers Phoebe and Hank?

20 What song was a hit for both Ray Stevens and Johnny Mathis?

46 All Those Years Ago

This quiz is about the singles and albums hits of 1986.

Who had these hit singles?

1   'Caravan Of Love'

2   'Manic Monday'

3   'Open Your Heart'

4   'Sometimes'

5   'On My Own'

6   'How Will I Know'

7   'Human'

8   'Sledgehammer'

9   'You Can Call Me Al'

10 'Sinful'

11 'Peter Gunn'

12 'Absolute Beginners'

13 'Panic'

14 'Some Candy Talking'

15 'Love Comes Quickly'
16 'Love Can't Turn Around'
17 'No One Is To Blame'
18 'Brilliant Mind'
19 'Rise'
20 'No More The Fool'
21 'Bizarre Love Triangle'
22 'Marlene On The Wall'
23 'Ain't Nothin' Going On But The Rent'
24 'Hounds Of Love'
25 'The Way It Is'

B

And these that were not such big hits?
1 'Driving Away From Home'
2 'Don't Walk'
3 'Come On Home'
4 'If You're Ready (Come Go With Me)'
5 'XX Sex'

And who hit with these albums?
6 *The Queen Is Dead*
7 *So*
8 *Revenge*
9 *Rapture*
10 *Control*
11 *Disco*

12 *Infected*
13 *Parade*
14 *Victorialand*
15 *Give Me The Reason*
16 *Who's Zoomin' Who*
17 *London 0 Hull 4*
18 *The Colour Of Spring*
19 *Listen Like Thieves*
20 *Black Celebration*
21 *Dirty Work*
22 *Invisible Touch*
23 *Big Cock*
24 *Slippery When Wet*
25 *True Blue*

C

1 Which single spent the longest in the charts in 1986?
2 On which number one album did Ladysmith Black Mambazo appear?
3 What did Sam Cooke, Marvin Gaye and Nick Kamen have in common?
4 An unprecedented event occurred on 12 July, when three new albums occupied the top three positions. Which albums?
5 Who were the producers of 'Chain Reaction'?
6 Which two acts had number ones with greatest hits packages?
7 In the singles chart, which two songs that hit the top had already enjoyed time there previously?
8 Who hit the Top Ten for the first time in 16½ years?
9 Which now incredibly successful duo's album debuted inauspiciously on 14 June?
10 Which two sisters were in the charts at the same time with different records?

11 Which album did *Brothers In Arms* keep at number two for five weeks?

12 Apart from Britain and America, five other countries were represented at number one in the singles chart. Name them and the acts involved.

13 Which record spent longest at number one in America?

14 Name the four EastEnders who hit the chart.

15 Who were John Crawford and Terri Nunn?

47 Word Up

In this quiz we present you with anagrams of the names of singers or bands. Fill the correct names in the boxes provided, and you will find that you have spelt out the name of another act by reading downwards in the marked boxes.

A

1	CRY, "O MIX US"	(4,5)
2	CLAY STRIKE	(4,6)
3	SEND SAM	(7)
4	SEND OUR NET	(10)
5	MANY A RUNG	(4,5)
6	JOLT ON, HEN	(5,4)
7	UP A BALLAD	(5,5)

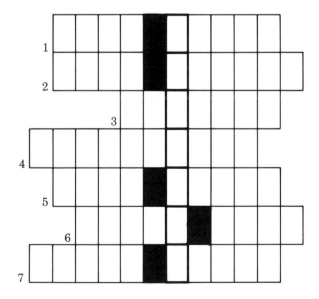

B

1 VEST STANCE   (3,7)
2 EEL PIE AGAIN   (6,5)
3 IN YOUTH SHE WON'T   (7,7)
4 CAN DRY FORWARD   (5,8)
5 FIT SAVER   (4,4)
6 GRAVY, I MEAN   (6,4)
7 DEALS   (5)
8 STRING ROAR   (5,5)

C

1 SHUT BEAK (4,4)
2 SOBBING CRY (4,6)
3 I LIKE 'EM YOUNG (5,7)
4 HOW (3)
5 CAT IN A TOMB (4,6)
6 I'M IN A ROLL (9)
7 DAN'S BARMEN (3,7)
8 TRIAD SISTER (4,7)

48 American Trilogy

This quiz tests your knowledge of American music and geography.

A

Fill in the missing American town or city in these song titles:

1 'Boy From _____ _____ City' – Darts
2 'Do You Know The Way To _____ _____' – Dionne Warwick
3 '_____' – Kiki Dee
4 'Angel Of _____' – U2
5 'The _____ _____ Run' – Carvells
6 '_____ Vice Theme' – Jan Hammer
7 'Battle Of _____ _____' – Lonnie Donegan
8 'Fairytale Of _____ _____' – Pogues
9 '_____' – Michelle Shocked
10 '_____ _____ (Be Sure To Wear Some Flowers In Your Hair)' –
    Scott Mackenzie
11 '_____ _____' – Tony Christie
12 'All The Way From _____' – Mott 'The Hoople
13 '_____' – Public Image Ltd
14 '_____ Freedom' – Elton John
15 'What Made _____ Famous' – Rod Stewart
16 '_____ City' – Little Richard
17 '_____ Skyline' – A-Ha
18 '_____ City' – Tom Jones
19 '_____ Cats' – Lovin' Spoonful
20 'From _____ _____ To _____ _____' Patsy Gallant

B

Can you name the state in which the following acts were born? It's not that hard if you think about it carefully – many artists write or sing songs about their birthplace.

1 Peter Cetera
2 Bruce Springsteen
3 Glenn Medeiros
4 Barbra Streisand
5 Donny Osmond
6 Tracy Chapman
7 George Benson
8 Elvis Presley
9 Prince
10 Dolly Parton
11 Glen Campbell
12 Gladys Knight

13 Michael Jackson
14 Madonna
15 Buddy Holly
16 Bobby Brown
17 Lionel Richie
18 Daryl Hall
19 Bruce Hornsby
20 Beach Boys

In America musical taste is quite different from the UK. The following songs all hit number one in the US by acts that were, or were to become, prominent in the UK, but none of these singles hit the British chart. They either flopped or were not released at all. Name the artists.

1 'The Long And Winding Road'
2 'I Write The Songs'
3 'Saturday Night'
4 'Fingertips (Part II)'
5 'Bad Blood'
6 'Half Breed'
7 'Thank God I'm A Country Boy'
8 'Rich Girl'
9 'Go Away Little Girl'
10 'He Don't Love You Like I Love You'
11 'I'm Henry VIII I Am'
12 'Thank You (Falettin Me Be Mice Elf Agin)'
13 'To Sir With Love'
14 'Love Is Thicker Than Water'
15 'Have You Ever Been Mellow'
16 'Jacob's Ladder'
17 'Shining Star'
18 'Best Of My Love'
19 'How Can You Mend A Broken Heart'
20 'The Sound Of Silence'

49 I'm Just A Singer (In A Rock 'N' Roll Band)

The limelight naturally falls on the vocalist of a group; many become just as well known as solo acts. Some, however, remain relatively anonymous. Can you name the group these singers front?

A

1 Marti Pellow
2 Jon Bon Jovi
3 Bono
4 Neil Tennant
5 Carol Decker
6 Matt Goss
7 Simon Le Bon
8 Chrissie Hynde
9 Andy Bell
10 Leee John
11 Mark King
12 Mick Hucknall
13 Morten Harket
14 Jim Kerr
15 Pete Burns
16 Simon Climie
17 Michael Hutchence
18 Phil Oakey
19 Roland Gift
20 Wendy James
21 Mark Shaw
22 Tony Hadley
23 Suggs
24 Buster Bloodvessel
25 Ben Volpeliere-Pierrot

B

Who are the lead singers with these groups?
1 Eurythmics
2 ABC
3 Guns N' Roses
4 Four Tops
5 New Order
6 Cameo
7 Style Council
8 Motorhead

9   Housemartins
10   Depeche Mode
11   Aswad
12   Sigue Sigue Sputnik
13   Cult
14   Pogues
15   Deacon Blue
16   Living In A Box
17   Aztec Camera
19   Fairground Attraction
20   Cure
21   Mission
22   Big Country
23   Iron Maiden
24   Slade
25   Scritti Politti

C

Again, which bands do or did these people lend their vocal talent to?

1   Mark Reilly
2   Tracy Thorn
3   Deiter Meier
4   David Glasper
5   Steve Tyler
6   Ian Brown
7   Iva Davies
8   Charlene Spittery
9   Mick Jones
10   Wayne Gidden
11   Bret Michaels
12   Mike Scott
13   Jaz Coleman
14   Mike Peters
15   Rita Ray
16   Andy Partridge
17   Geddy Lee
18   Gabriele Kerner
19   Miles Hunt
20   Joey Tempest
21   Gary Daly
22   Peter Noone
23   Peter Cox
24   Corrinne Drewery
25   Brian Setzer

50 The Final Countdown

This is the 50th and last quiz. To complete this one, you will have to flick back through the pages and look at the titles of the 50 quizzes, which you will notice are all song titles. Try to name the artists most associated with the songs used as titles, and award yourself one point for each correct answer.

1 First Picture Of You
2 Miss You Like Crazy
3 The Oldest Swinger In Town
4 Who Killed Bambi?
5 If I Said You Had A Beautiful Body, Would You Hold It Against Me?
6 Detroit City
7 Brothers In Arms
8 No Particular Place To Go
9 Dress You Up
10 Cover Me
11 Put It There
12 Band On The Run
13 Lady Madonna
14 The Politics Of Dancing
15 Coming Around Again
16 Monkey
17 The Name Of The Game
18 Everything Starts With An 'E'
19 In A Big Country
20 The Road To Nowhere
21 Girl Crazy
22 One Two Three O'Leary
23 Time (Clock Of The Heart)
24 American Pie
25 Cross The Track (We Better Go Back)

26 Two Out Of Three Ain't Bad
27 Madchester Rave On
28 Green Onions
29 Leave Me Alone
30 Sing Our Own Song
31 Laugh At Me
32 Year Of Decision
33 Panic
34 Little Things Mean A Lot
35 The Big One
36 I'd Rather Jack
37 Starman
38 Si Si Je Suis Un Rock Star
39 Michael Jackson Medley
40 Nice Legs Shame About The Face
41 Song Sung Blue
42 Food For Thought
43 The Letter
44 Calling Your Name
45 Sunshine On Leith
46 All Those Years Ago
47 Word Up
48 American Trilogy
49 I'm Just A Singer (In A Rock 'N' Roll Band)
50 The Final Countdown

1 First Picture Of You

A

1	Abba	14	Dire Straits
2	Sex Pistols	15	Whitney Houston
3	Toyah	16	Queen
4	Bucks Fizz	17	Boney M
5	Soft Cell	18	Elvis Presley
6	Pet Shop Boys	19	Madonna
7	Roxy Music	20	David Bowie
8	Bob Marley	21	Gary Numan
9	Kylie Minogue	22	Status Quo
10	Culture Club	23	Police
11	Frankie Goes To Hollywood	24	Rick Astley
12	Wham!	25	Elton John
13	Phil Collins		

B

1	Beach Boys	14	Jam
2	Stranglers	15	Shakin' Stevens
3	Peter Gabriel	16	Iron Maiden
4	Chris De Burgh	17	Diana Ross
5	Genesis	18	Marvin Gaye
6	Depeche Mode	19	Madness
7	Rolling Stones	20	Chris Rea
8	Clash	21	U2 (or Crazy World of Arthur
9	Beatles		Brown)
10	Bruce Springsteen	22	Natalie Cole
11	Dexy's Midnight Runners	23	Paul Hardcastle
12	Fleetwood Mac	24	Hollies
13	Pretenders	25	Human League

C

1	INXS	14	New Order
2	Bon Jovi	15	Hazell Dean
3	Housemartins	16	Black Lace
4	Level 42	17	Blancmange
5	Erasure	18	AC/DC
6	Pogues	19	Cure
7	Altered Images	20	Chas and Dave
8	Soul II Soul	21	Aswad
9	Randy Crawford	22	Kane Gang
10	Def Leppard	23	Robert Palmer
11	Foreigner	24	Orchestral Manoeuvres In The
12	Echo and the Bunnymen		Dark
13	Simple Minds	25	Marillion

2   Miss You Like Crazy

A

1	House	11	Town
2	Party	12	Life
3	Talk	13	Japanese
4	Heaven	14	Hand
5	Jack	15	Tiger
6	Girls	16	Heat
7	Alone	17	Tokyo
8	Children	18	California
9	Cruel	19	On
10	Under	20	Everybody

B

1	Band	11	Cut
2	Purple	12	Road
3	Nothing	13	Heart
4	Songs	14	Black
5	Big	15	Tonight
6	Out	16	Beatles
7	Fish	17	Love
8	Wheels	18	Soul
9	War	19	W.
10	One	20	Crazy

C

1	Richard	11	Talking
2	Glitter	12	Wilson
3	Murray	13	Lee
4	Force	14	Jackson
5	Wayne	15	James
6	Roxanne	16	Brothers
7	Pink	17	Pop
8	Cliff	18	Wonder
9	Hollywood	19	George
10	Michael	20	Kelly

3 The Oldest Swinger In Town

A

1	Smokey Robinson	14	Merrill Osmond
2	Joe Cocker	15	Andy Stewart
3	Billy Joel	16	Frank Sinatra
4	Barry Gibb	17	Eartha Kitt
5	Jason Donovan	18	Vangelis
6	Johnny Mathis	19	Barry White
7	Petula Clark	20	George Harrison
8	Herbie Hancock	21	Tammy Wynette
9	Ringo Starr	22	Olivia Newton-John
10	Ian Gillan	23	Placido Domingo
11	Leonard Cohen	24	Perry Como
12	Lionel Richie	25	Dana
13	Jermaine Jackson		

B

1	Thomas Dolby	14	Meat Loaf
2	Holly Johnson	15	Deborah Harry
3	Sade	16	Bryan Ferry
4	Billy Bragg	17	James Brown
5	Anita Baker	18	Ella Fitzgerald
6	Terence Trent D'Arby	19	Roberta Flack
7	Debbie Gibson	20	Gary Glitter
8	Natalie Cole	21	Bill Wyman
9	Randy Crawford	22	George Benson
10	David Cassidy	23	Barbra Streisand
11	Bruce Springsteen	24	Malcolm McLaren
12	Alexander O'Neal	25	Joni Mitchell
13	Shakin' Stevens		

C

1	1929	14	1951
2	1958	15	1946
3	1961	16	1956
4	1958	17	1942
5	1968	18	1936
6	1938	19	1946
7	1953	20	1947
8	1948	21	1963
9	1933	22	1966
10	1933	23	1949
11	1941	24	1958
12	1959	25	1966
13	1955		

4 Who Killed Bambi?

A

1 Jive Bunny and the Mastermixers
2 'Nellie The Elephant'
3 Tight Fit
4 'Fox On The Run'
5 Curiosity Killed The Cat
6 Roland Rat Superstar
7 Eagles
8 Adam & the Ants
9 Chas & Dave
10 'Buffalo Stance'
11 Mud
12 Survivor
13 Spitting Image
14 Paul McCartney
15 Terence Trent D'Arby
16 Blow Monkeys
17 Fleetwood Mac
18 'Birdie Song (Birdie Dance)'
19 Cat Stevens
20 Def Leppard

B

1 Cure
2 Boomtown Rats
3 A lion
4 Donny Osmond
5 David Cassidy
6 Samantha Fox
7 a) horse
8 b) cow
9 1967
10 Stray Cats
11 'Rat In Mi Kitchen'
12 Meatloaf
13 Pet Shop Boys
14 Paul McCartney
15 Creatures
16 Animals
17 John Lennon
18 'Elusive Butterfly'
19 *Watership Down*
20 '(How Much Is) That Doggie In The Window'

C

1 'Pickin' A Chicken'
2 Three Dog Night
3 'Joy To The World'
4 Black Gorilla
5 *Seven And The Ragged Tiger*
6 Yellow Dog
7 Goons
8 Crickets
9 'Yakety Yak'
10 Norma Tanega
11 Bow Wow Wow
12 Chicken Shack
13 Yardbirds
14 Los Lobos
15 David Thorne
16 Thrashing Doves
17 'I Ran'
18 Silent Underdog (aka Paul Hardcastle)
19 Not the Nine O'Clock News Cast
20 Captain Beaky And His Band

5 If I Said You Had A Beautiful Body, Would You Hold It Against Me

A

1	Divine	11	Prince
2	Gary Glitter	12	Elton John
3	Carly Simon	13	ABC
4	Kid Creole And The Coconuts	14	Sinitta
5	Fern Kinney or Steve Allan	15	Diana Ross
6	Temptations or Aswad	16	Pee Bee Squad
7	Hot Chocolate	17	Hugo Montenegro
8	Ken Mackintosh	18	Psychedelic Furs
9	Sparks	19	U2
10	Rod Stewart	20	Bimbo Jet

B

1 'My Eyes Adored You' – Frankie Valli
2 'Feet Up' – Guy Mitchell
3 'Lucky Lips' – Cliff Richard
4 'Let Me Cry On Your Shoulder' – Ken Dodd
4 'Perfect Skin' – Lloyd Cole and the Commotions
6 'Fattie Bum Bum' – Carl Malcolm or the Diversions
7 'She's Got Claws' – Gary Numan
8 'Never Turn Your Back On Mother Earth' – Sparks
9 'Nipple To The Bottle' – Grace Jones
10 'Third Finger, Left Hand' – Pearls
11 'Thighs High (Grip Your Hips And Move)' – Tom Browne
12 'Big Mouth Strikes Again' – Smiths
13 'Head Over Heels' – Kevin Keegan
14 'Wear My Ring Around Your Neck' – Elvis Presley
15 'Heart Of Glass' – Blondie
16 'When The Girl In Your Arms Is The Girl In Your Heart' – Cliff Richard
17 'Under Your Thumb' – Godley And Creme
18 'Losing My Mind' – Liza Minnelli
19 'Knee Deep In The Blues' – Guy Mitchell or Tommy Steele
20 'Mistletoe And Wine' – Cliff Richard

C

1 Billy Bragg
2 'Pretty Young Thing'
3 Michael Jackson sang about a 'Man In The Mirror', the Human League about a 'Mirror Man'
4 'Blondes Have More Fun'
5 Nile Rodgers
6 'Physical' by Olivia Newton-John
7 'I Want Your Sex' by George Michael
8 *Lexicon Of Love* by ABC
9 'She's A Bad Mama Jama (She's Built, She's Stacked)'
10 Stray Cats

6 Detroit City

A

1 'I Just Called to Say I Love You'
2 *What's Going On* by Marvin Gaye
3 The Supremes
4 Shorty Long
5 'Reet Petite'
6 The Carpenters
7 Marvin Gaye
8 Levi Stubbs
9 Martha and the Vandellas
10 'I've Never Been To Me'
11 Diana Ross
12 Tammi Terrell
13 The Vandellas
14 Smokey Robinson and the Miracles
15 'Got To Be There'
16 'Twenty-Five Miles'
17 The Commodores
18 Holland–Dozier–Holland
19 *Lady Sings The Blues*
20 Jimmy Ruffin

B

1 The Velvelettes
2 'This Old Heart of Mine'
3 *Natural High* by the Commodores
4 Rare Earth
5 'Reach Out I'll Be There' ('Baby Love' had appeared on Stateside.)
6 'Where Did Our Love Go' and 'I Can't Help Myself'
7 O'Kelly, Ronald and Rudolph
8 Rick James, working outside Motown, produced the hit for the US Columbia label.
9 'I'm Gonna Make You Love Me'
10 'Do You Love Me'
11 The Mary Jane Girls
12 Mowest
13 Brenda Holloway
14 Gladys Knight and the Pips
15 'You Got What It Takes'
16 Motor Town
17 The Rev. Martin Luther King Jr.
18 *Endless Love*
19 The Temptations
20 Mary Wells

C

1 Johnny Gill
2 'Reflections'
3 Tom Clay
4 Diana Ross
5 The Vancouvers
6 'Money'
7 The Undisputed Truth
8 *Little Stevie Wonder/The 12 Year Old Genius*
9 Canadian
10 Berry Gordy Sr.
11 Teena Marie
12 Rick James
13 *Motown Chartbusters Volume 3*
14 The Four Tops
15 *Where Did Our Love Go* by the Supremes
16 Kiki Dee
17 Sam Harris
18 Stoney
19 Jackie, Jermaine, Marlon, Michael and Tito
20 The Temptations

7 Brothers In Arms

A

1 Bros
2 Everly Brothers
3 Spandau Ballet
4 Bee Gees
5 Jackson Five
6 Jacksons
7 Dire Straits
8 Kool and the Gang
9 Kinks
10 UB40
11 Beach Boys
12 New Kids On The Block

B

1 Osmonds
2 Christians
3 Sparks
4 Clannad
5 Undertones or That Petrol Emotion
6 Hue And Cry
7 Japan
8 INXS
9 Earth Wind And Fire
10 Musical Youth
11 Level 42
12 Van Halen

C

1 Gipsy Kings
2 Happy Mondays
3 Prefab Sprout
4 Real Thing
5 A Flock Of Seagulls
6 Proclaimers
7 Danny Wilson
8 Bachelors
9 Colourbox or M/A/R/R/S
10 Psychedelic Furs
11 Neville Brothers
12 Ziggy Marley and the Melody Makers

8 No Particular Place To Go

A

1	Ethiopia	12	Chuck Berry
2	Don McLean's	13	Elvis Presley
3	'Belfast Child'	14	Paul Simon
4	Bee Gees	15	Jam
5	'Africa'	16	Lisa Stansfield
6	'Walking On The Moon'	17	'San Francisco (Be Sure To
7	The Pogues		Wear Some Flowers In Your
8	'Letter From America'		Hair)'
9	Europe	18	Clash
10	Abba	19	Then Jerico
11	'Baker Street'	20	Bay City Rollers

B

1	Manhattan Transfer	11	Billy Joel
2	Greece	12	'Lost In France'
3	Venice	13	Dutch
4	'Cambodia'	14	Germany
5	David Essex	15	Japan
6	London Boys	16	'The Amsterdam EP'
7	Murray Head	17	Boney M
8	Number two	18	'California Girls'
9	Prefab Sprout	19	Julie Covington
10	Mica Paris	20	'French Kissin' In The USA'

C

1	Frankie Goes To Hollywood	12	Venice In Peril
2	Latin Quarter	13	'Greetings From Asbury Park,
3	'Winchester Cathedral'		N.J.'
4	Wigan's Chosen Few	14	'Nebraska'
5	'A Walk In The Black Forest'	15	Stranglers
6	Japan	16	Canada
7	Jimmie Rodgers	17	Siouxsie & the Banshees
8	Red Box	18	Roger Miller
9	'Boston Tea Party'	19	Lonnie Donegan
10	China Crisis	20	Iceland
11	Frank Sinatra		

9 Dress You Up

A

1	Troosers	11	Shawl
2	Hat	12	Trousers
3	Boots	13	Pants
4	Glove	14	Boots
5	Jeans	15	Dress
6	Shoes	16	Coat
7	Shirts	17	Shirt
8	Hats	18	Shoes
9	Shoes	19	Fly
10	Jacket	20	Knickers

B

1	Blue	11	Silver
2	Green	12	Black
3	Blue	13	Red
4	Raspberry	14	Scarlet
5	Blue	15	Yellow
6	Green	16	Shakin' Stevens
7	White	17	George Shearing
8	Sky Blue and Rainbow	18	Chris Farlowe
9	White	19	Elvis Presley
10	White	20	Tracey Ullman

C

1 Tony Bennett, Elvis Presley or David Whitfield
2 'Ally's Tartan Army'
3 'Lucy In The Sky With Diamonds'
4 Marmalade
5 Brutus Jeans
6 'The Future's So Bright I Gotta Wear Shades'
7 Paul Gardiner (although Gary Numan did the vocals on 'Stormtrooper In Drag')
8 'Shoes'
9 Don Henley's ('Dirty Laundry')
10 Cream
11 Gary Byrd and the GB Experience
12 ZZ Top
13 Midge Ure and Mick Karn
14 'Brilliant Disguise'
15 Gang Of Four
16 Iron Maiden or the Skyhooks, who both hit with 'Women In Uniform'
17 'Lipstick On Your Collar'
18 'Pyjamarama'
19 Bill Wyman
20 'Nights In White Satin'

10 Cover Me

1 *The Sensual World* – Kate Bush
2 *Upstairs At Eric's* – Yazoo
3 *Hatful Of Hollow* – The Smiths
4 *Business As Usual* – Men At Work
5 *Boy* – U2
6 *Rio* – Duran Duran
7 *Ghost In The Machine* – The Police
8 *The Who Sell Out* – The Who
9 *Lovesexy* – Prince
10 *Abbey Road* – The Beatles
11 *Club Classics Vol. One* – Soul II Soul
12 *True Blue* – Madonna
13 *Sparkle In The Rain* – Simple Minds
14 *Tango In The Night* – Fleetwood Mac
15 *Transformer* – Lou Reed
16 *Hunky Dory* – David Bowie
17 *Original Soundtrack* – S Express
18 *Dark Side Of The Moon* – Pink Floyd
19 *Born In The USA* – Bruce Springsteen
20 *Brothers In Arms* – Dire Straits

11 Put It There

A

1 Biros (Bros)
2 New Skids On The Block (New Kids On The Block)
3 Stalking Heads (Talking Heads)
4 Midget Ure (Midge Ure)
5 Pest Shop Boys (Pet Shop Boys)
6 Skate Bush (Kate Bush)
7 Simply Bred (Simply Red)
8 A-Hat (A-Ha)
9 Skim Wilde (Kim Wilde)
10 Nike and Tina Turner (Ike and Tina Turner)
11 Jimmy Snail (Jimmy Nail)
12 Flat Boys (Fat Boys)
13 Brick Astley (Rick Astley)
14 Five Start (Five Star)
15 Graze (Raze)

B

1 Pal Martino (Al Martino)
2 Hanky Marvin (Hank Marvin)
3 Wall About Eve (All About Eve)
4 Pram Jam (Ram Jam)
5 Jesse Rage (Jesse Rae)
6 Bald Company (Bad Company)
7 Mighty Wash (Mighty Wah)
8 Chasm and Dave (Chas and Dave)
9 Rash Band (Rah Band)
10 Randy Kim (Andy Kim)
11 Vicehouse (Icehouse)
12 Huey Lewis and the Newts (Huey Lewis and the News)
13 Roland Prat Superstar (Roland Rat Superstar)
14 Kenya (Enya)
15 Wart (War)

C

1 Ninja and Frederick (Nina and Frederick)
2 Mean To Man (Man To Man)
3 Tit Bites (It Bites)
4 New Model Barmy (New Model Army)
5 Nun Shooz (Nu Shooz)
6 Spam Hall (Pam Hall)
7 Huge and Cry (Hue and Cry)
8 Richie Reich (Richie Rich)
9 Keen Dodd (Ken Dodd)
10 Spat and Mick (Pat and Mick)
11 Prose Royce (Rose Royce)
12 Movie (Move)
13 Shame 69 (Sham 69)
14 Drainmakers (Rainmakers)
15 Bring Crosby (Bing Crosby)

12 Band On The Run

A

1 Paul McCartney
2 Graham Nash
3 Jimmy Somerville
4 Eric Clapton
5 Norman Cook
6 David Sylvian
7 Ryuichi Sakamoto
8 Ron Wood
9 Annie Lennox
10 John Lydon (Johnny Rotten)
11 Paul Weller
12 Vince Clarke
13 George Harrison
14 Marc Almond
15 George Michael
16 Ritchie Blackmore
17 Ringo Starr
18 Paul Simon and Art Garfunkel
19 Phil Fearon
20 Terry Hall

B

1 Kenny Jones
2 Martin Ware and Ian Craig Marsh
3 Sarah Dallin and Keren ' Woodward of Bananarama – that's all
4 Greg Lake
5 Vince Clarke
6 Christine McVie
7 Tom McGuinness
8 Jeff Lynne
9 Paul Carrack
10 Tony James
11 June Miles-Kingston
12 Midge Ure
13 Denny Laine
14 Lemmy
15 Johnny Marr
16 Jimmy Page
17 Steve Winwood
18 Cass Elliott
19 Roy Wood
20 Andy Summers

C

1 Nile Rodgers
2 Gary Tibbs
3 Kenny Rogers
4 Eric Stewart
5 Roy Hay
6 Peter Frampton
7 Graham Gouldman
8 Terry Sylvester
9 Aynsley Dunbar
10 Clem Cattini and Alan Caddy
11 Jeff Lynne
12 Gary Brooker, and, sort of, Robin Trower
13 Gerry Rafferty
14 Ray St. John
15 Frank Allen
16 Brian Bennett
17 Rod Stewart
18 Cindy Birdsong
19 Jim Peterik
20 Andy Connell

13 Lady Madonna

A

1 'Into The Groove'
2 'Holiday'
3 'La Isla Bonita'
4 'Material Girl'
5 'Vogue'
6 'Papa Don't Preach'
7 'Like A Prayer'
8 'Who's That Girl'
9 'True Blue'
10 'Lucky Star'

B

1 'Causing A Commotion'
2 'Like A Virgin'
3 'Dress You Up'
4 'Dear Jessie'
5 'I Know It'
6 'Express Yourself'
7 'Borderline'
8 'Open Your Heart'
9 'Live To Tell'
10 'Cherish'

C

1 'Gambler'
2 'White Heat'
3 'The Look Of Love'
4 'Keep It Together'
5 'Angel'
6 'Shoo-Bee-Doo'
7 'Pretender'
8 'Supernatural'
9 'Jimmy Jimmy'
10 'Where's The Party'

14 The Politics Of Dancing

A

1	John Lennon	12	10 C.C.
2	Paul McCartney	13	'A Little Peace'
3	George Harrison	14	Arcadia
4	Ringo Starr	15	Duran Duran
5	Specials	16	'A New England'
6	Peter Gabriel	17	'In The Ghetto'
7	Phil Collins	18	'Ghost Town'
8	'19'	19	'Another Brick In The Wall (Part II)'
9	Sex Pistols		
10	Sex Pistols	20	*Evita*
11	'Two Tribes'		

B

1	Bob Dylan	11	Stevie Wonder
2	Joan Baez	12	Jimi Hendrix
3	Boy George	13	Country Joe and the Fish
4	The Beat	14	Big Audio Dynamite
5	'Soweto'	15	Strawbs
6	Tracy Chapman	16	Sting
7	Barry McGuire	17	Billy Bragg
8	Edwin Starr	18	'Elected'
9	Scritti Politti	19	Clash
10	'Masterblaster (Jammin')' by Stevie Wonder	20	Spitting Image

C

1	Mike Curb	11	'Mr. President'
2	Charles Gates Dawes	12	Dion
3	Joyce Blair (Lionel Blair's sister)	13	'Black And White'
4	Sir Winston Churchill	14	Groundhogs
5	Dead Kennedys	15	The Miners' Strike of 1984
6	China Crisis	16	'Banana Republic' by the Boomtown Rats.
7	Peter Sellers	17	Big Daddy
8	Clash	18	Prefab Sprout
9	Malcolm X	19	*1984*
10	*Cry Freedom*	20	Bob Marley

15 Coming Around Again

A

1. Levi jeans
2. Miller Lite Lager
3. Nescafé Coffee
4. Renault Cars
5. Ford Cars
6. Pretty Polly Tights
7. Halifax Building Society
8. Public Health Campaign
9. Right Guard Deodorant
10. Start Breakfast Cereal

B

1 It was first used as a TV theme tune and was then re-issued in aid of the Zeebrugge Ferry Disaster Fund
2 'Love Me Do'
3 '(Just Like) Starting Over', 'Imagine' and 'Woman'
4 1980, '81, '82, '83, '84, '85, '86
5 *Good Morning Vietnam*
6 Eight
7 'This Brutal House'
8 It was heavily sampled in S Express' number one hit 'Theme From S Express'
9 Jam
10 'Life Is A Dance'

C

1 Ben Liebrand
2 Stock Aitken Waterman
3 Peter Slaghuis
4 Patrick Cowley
5 Ben Liebrand, again
6 Danny D. of D. Mob
7 Simon Harris
8 John Rocca
9 Arthur Baker
10 Ben Liebrand, yet again

16 Monkey

A   Pebbles
B   Art
C   Up Up and Away
D   Later in the Evening
E   Start
F   I Wish
G   Mojo
H   Oh
I   Nova
J   Terror
K   Hearts And Bones
L   Echo
M   Bright
N   Ochs
O   Yum Yum
P   It's Hard
Q   Nico
R   The Best
S   Hejira
T   Empty
U   Baby
V   Uptight
W   Batman
X   Bird
Y   Lace
Z   Eat It
AA Studio

The quoted song is 'The Boy in the Bubble' by Paul Simon. 'It's a turn-around jump shot / It's everybody jump start / It's every generation throws a hero up the pop charts / Medicine is magical and magical is art / The Boy in the Bubble / And the baby with the baboon heart' Words by Paul Simon, Copyright Paul Simon.

ITS A TURN-AROUND

JUMP SHOT

ITS EVERYBODY JUMP

START

ITS EVERY GENERATION

THROWS A HERO UP

THE POP CHARTS

MEDICINE IS MAGICAL

AND MAGICAL IS ART

THE BOY IN THE

BUBBLE

AND THE BABY WITH

THE BABOON HEART

17 The Name Of The Game

A

1	Pearson	11	Berry
2	Goss	12	King
3	Jackson	13	James
4	Osmond	14	Marie
5	Brown	15	Hall
6	Gibb	16	Miller
7	Jones	17	Nelson
8	Jones	18	Nolan
9	Jackson	19	Johnson
10	Grant	20	O'Connor

B

1	Paul	11	Tom
2	George	12	Chris
3	David	13	Brenda
4	Don	14	Kim
5	Gary	15	Linda
6	Debbie	16	Tracey
7	Roger	17	Keith
8	Bruce	18	Andy
9	Billy	19	Jennifer
10	Grace	20	Joe

C

1	Modern
2	New
3	Jack
4	Three
5	Real
6	Red
7	Singing
8	Gang
9	Dirty
10	Jesus
11	King
12	Christmas
13	House
14	Sally
15	Don't
16	Good
17	Julie
18	Johnny
19	Love
20	Baby

18 Everything Starts With An 'E'

A

1 Enya
2 Erasure
3 'Every Loser Wins'
4 Eurythmics
5 Gloria Estefan & Miami Sound Machine
6 Stevie Wonder
7 Kylie Minogue
8 Electronic
9 Big Audio Dynamite
10 Electric Light Orchestra
11 'Especially For You'
12 Everly Brothers
13 Rolling Stones
14 'Enjoy The Silence'
15 Kenny Everett
16 England World Cup Squad
17 'Everything I Own'
18 Police
19 Philip Bailey
20 'Easy Lover'

B

1 Europe
2 'Enola Gay'
3 Echo & the Bunnymen
4 Dave Edmunds
5 Duane Eddy
6 Eighth Wonder
7 Eddy Grant
8 Equals
9 Everything But The Girl
10 David Essex
11 'Escape (The Pina Colada Song)'
12 Eagles
13 'Love Grows (Where My Rosemary Goes)'
14 Sheena Easton
15 'Eye Of The Tiger'
16 Milkman
17 Easybeats
18 'A Date With Elvis'
19 Everton F.C.
20 'Eleanor Rigby'

C

1 Shirley Ellis
2 Billy Eckstine
3 Sheila E
4 Emerald Express
5 Easybeats
6 Ensign
7 'Waterloo' by Abba
8 Ex Pistols
9 Evangel Temple Choir
10 *Expresso Bongo*
11 Phil Everly
12 'Empty Garden'
13 Edelweiss – 'Bring Me Edelweiss'
14 'Eloise'
15 Eruption
16 'Eye Level' by the Simon Park Orchestra
17 Exile
18 'Eliminator'
19 Paul Evans
20 Bern Elliott and the Fenmen

19 In A Big Country

A

1	Sweden and Norway	11	Canada
2	Australia	12	Greece
3	Ireland	13	Guyana
4	Switzerland	14	Jamaica
5	Belgium	15	France
6	Italy	16	Japan
7	France and Germany	17	Iceland
8	Norway	18	Germany
9	Spain	19	Australia
10	Israel	20	Ireland

B

1 American
2 Swiss
3 China
4 Jamaican
5 Japanese
6 Spanish
7 Indian
8 English
9 Brazilian
10 Haitian
11 Portuguese
12 German
13 Argentine
14 Swedish
15 Egyptian
16 French
17 Scottish
18 Irish
19 Bermuda
20 Turkey

C

1 Luxembourg
2 'Je T'Aime . . . Moi Non Plus' by Jane Birkin and Serge Gainsbourg
3 Black Box, Starlight and Mixmaster
4 Falco
5 St. Kitts
6 KOHYEPT
7 Izhar Cohen and Alphabeta, and Milk and Honey
8 1980
9 Polish, Matt Bianco
10 'Sukiyaki' by Kyu Sakamoto, and also by Kenny Ball and his Jazzmen

20 The Road To Nowhere

A

Sandie Shaw recorded 'Hand In Glove' written and produced by the **Smiths**: Johnny Marr of the Smiths was a member of **Electronic**: so was Neil Tennant of the **Pet Shop Boys**: the Pet Shop Boys produced and duetted with **Dusty Springfield** on various late Eighties hits: Dusty and **Mike Hurst** were both members of the Springfields: Hurst produced the Manfred Mann version of '**The Mighty Quinn**': 'The Mighty Quinn' and '**All I Really Want To Do**' were written by Bob Dylan: **Cher** had a hit with her version of 'All I Really Want To Do': Cher duetted with **Meatloaf** on his hit 'Dead Ringer': it was produced by **Jim Steinman**: so was **Bonnie Tyler**'s 'Total Eclipse Of The Heart': Bonnie teamed up with **Shakin' Stevens** on 'A Rockin' Good Way': Shaky had a hit with his version of the **Gary Glitter** hit, 'A Little Boogie Woogie (In The Back Of My Mind)': most of Glitter's hits were co-written and produced by **Mike Leander**: Leander and his partner Eddie Seago wrote and produced **Tom Jones**' 1987 hit single 'A Boy From Nowhere': Tom Jones and Art Of Noise hit with **Prince**'s 'Kiss': Prince wrote 'I Feel For You', **Chaka Khan**'s number one: Chaka duetted with **Ray Charles** on the Quincy Jones hit, 'I'll Be Good To You': Ray Charles appeared in the film *The Blues Brothers*: the Blues Brothers version of 'Everybody Needs Somebody To Love' was sampled heavily on **Jive Bunny**'s fourth hit, 'Sounds Good To Me'

B

Sandie Shaw was discovered by **Adam Faith**: Adam starred with **David Essex** in the film *That'll Be The Day*: Essex starred with **Sinitta** in his London musical *Mutiny*: Sinitta and **Robert Knight** both hit with 'Love On A Mountain Top': Robert Knight recorded the original version of **Love Affair**'s number one, 'Everlasting Love': **Mike Smith** (not the radio and TV man) produced it: he also produced **Marmalade**'s 'Ob-La-Di Ob-La-Da' chart-topper: that came from the album *The Beatles*: **Paul McCartney**, who wrote 'Ob-La-Di Ob-La-Da' with John Lennon, was a Beatle: McCartney duetted with **Michael Jackson** on two Top Ten hits: Jackson and **Diana Ross** appeared together in the film, *The Wiz* and have sung together often: Ross and **Marvin Gaye** had two hit duets in 1974: Marvin Gaye and **Mary Wells** had one week at number 50 together with 'Once Upon A Time' in 1964: Mary Wells' hit 'My Guy' was covered in a medley of 'My Guy – My Girl' by **Amii Stewart and Johnny Bristol**: Bristol wrote the **Osmonds**' number one 'Love Me For A Reason': that hit was produced by **Mike Curb**: Curb went on to become Lieutenant Governor of California: another notable California politician was Mayor **Clint Eastwood** of Carmel: Clint's only UK single hit was 'I Talk The Trees', on the B-side of **Lee Marvin**'s number one 'Wandrin' Star'

C

Marianne Faithfull was at one stage a close friend of **Mick Jagger**: Jagger and Wood are both **Rolling Stones**: **Ron Wood** was previously a member of the **Faces**: **Rod Stewart** was their lead vocalist: Stewart and **B. A. Robertson** have both been involved in Scotland World Cup singles: Robertson also duetted with Frida of **Abba** on the smallish hit 'Time' at the end of 1983: Abba won the Eurovision Song Contest, as did **Sandie Shaw**: Sandie began her chart career with a cover of **Dionne Warwick**'s US smash '(There's) Always Something There To Remind Me': **Elton John** was one of Dionne's "Friends" on the AIDS charity hit,

'That's What Friends Are For': Elton and **Cliff Richard** duetted on the hit single 'Slow Rivers' in 1986: Cliff and **Sarah Brightman** hit the Top Ten in 1986 with 'All I Ask Of You': Sarah Brightman and **Jimmy Somerville** have both had chart duets with members of the Miles-Kingston clan, Sarah with Paul and Jimmy with June: Somerville has used parts of two **Donna Summer** hits in his own chart career, 'I Feel Love' as part of Bronski Beat with Marc Almond, and 'No More Tears (Enough Is Enough)' as a soloist: Donna Summer is one of the many acts providing Top Ten hits for the production team of **Stock Aitken Waterman**: **Bananarama** is another: Bananarama's first two chart appearances were with **Fun Boy Three**: Fun Boy Three were survivors from the break-up of the **Specials**: the Specials wrote and hit with the anthem **'Nelson Mandela'**: and **Tracy Chapman** first came to prominence at Nelson Mandela's 70th Birthday Concert in 1988

21 Girl Crazy

A

1	Dexy's Midnight Runners	12	Johnny Ray
2	Kenny Rogers	13	Overlanders
3	Harry Belafonte and Boney M	14	Everly Brothers
4	Paul Anka	15	Gilbert O'Sullivan
5	Bachelors	16	Slim Whitman
6	Everly Brothers	17	Royal Scots Dragoon Guards and the Tymes
7	Shakin' Stevens		
8	Four Pennies	18	Ricky Valance
9	Rod Stewart	19	Michael Jackson
10	Scaffold	20	Beatles
11	John Denver		

B

1	Pearl	11	Olwen
2	Bridget	12	Sheila
3	Patti	13	Linda
4	Petula	14	Joanie
5	Edie	15	Jonee
6	Leyna	16	Bette
7	Bonnie	17	Tina
8	Rosalie	18	Hazel
9	Suzanne	19	Marianne
10	Rhonda	20	Judy

C

1	Ruby	11	Sally
2	Charlotte	12	Marie
3	Annie	13	Sue
4	Betty	14	Bernadette
5	Cindy	15	Jane
6	Delilah	16	Joanna
7	Carrie	17	Lucy
8	Mary	18	Mandy
9	Jennifer	19	Alice
10	Rosie	20	Martha

22 One Two Three O'Leary

A

1 *Songs From The Big Chair* – Tears For Fears
2 *Pet Shop Boys, Actually* – Pet Shop Boys
3 *Bad* – Michael Jackson
4 *Tracy Chapman* – Tracy Chapman
5 *A New Flame* – Simply Red
6 *Kylie* – Kylie Minogue
7 *Rattle And Hum* – U2
8 *Stronger* – Cliff Richard
9 *Hangin' Tough* – New Kids On The Block
10 *I Do Not Want What I Haven't Got* – Sinead O'Connor
11 *Graceland* – Paul Simon
12 *We Too Are One* – Eurythmics
13 *Sergeant Pepper's Lonely Hearts Club Band* – Beatles
14 *War Of The Worlds* – Jeff Wayne/Various Artists
15 *Brothers In Arms* – Dire Straits
16 *. . . But Seriously* – Phil Collins
17 *Thriller* – Michael Jackson
18 *Affection* – Lisa Stansfield
19 *Kick* – INXS
20 *Like A Prayer* – Madonna

B

1 *Keep Your Distance* – Curiosity Killed The Cat
2 *Rio* – Duran Duran
3 *World Machine* – Level 42
4 *The Seeds Of Love* – Tears For Fears
5 *Blast* – Holly Johnson
6 *Heaven On Earth* – Belinda Carlisle
7 *Martika* – Martika
8 *Bridge Of Spies* – T'Pau
9 *First Of A Million Kisses* – Fairground Attraction
10 *Welcome To The Beautiful South* – Beautiful South
11 *Foreign Affair* – Tina Turner
12 *Volume One* – Traveling Wilburys
13 *Rubber Soul* – Beatles
14 *Scary Monsters And Super Creeps* – David Bowie
15 *Love Over Gold* – Dire Straits
16 *Rumours* – Fleetwood Mac
17 *Pipes Of Peace* – Paul McCartney
18 *Like A Virgin* – Madonna
19 *Dancing On The Ceiling* – Lionel Richie
20 *Bridge Over Troubled Water* – Simon And Garfunkel

C

1 *Turn Back The Clock* – Johnny Hates Jazz
2 *Love* – Aztec Camera
3 *Get Even* – Brother Beyond
4 *Short Sharp Shocked* – Michelle Shocked
5 *Back On The Block* – Quincy Jones
6 *The Other Side Of The Mirror* – Stevie Nicks
7 *Highway 61 Revisited* – Bob Dylan
8 *Spike* – Elvis Costello
9 *Please Please Me* –Beatles
10 *City To City* – Gerry Rafferty
11 *Pet Sounds* – Beach Boys
12 *Spirits Having Flown* – Bee Gees
13 *The Kick Inside* – Kate Bush
14 *Cosmo's Factory* – Creedence Clearwater Revival
15 *Ice On Fire* – Elton John
16 *Outlandos D'Amour* – Police
17 *A Date With Elvis* – Elvis Presley
18 *Jazz* – Queen
19 *Tattoo You* – Rolling Stones
20 *Wonderful Life* – Black

23 Time (Clock Of The Heart)

A

1	Boomtown Rats	11	Blondie
2	Alexander O'Neal	12	Shalamar
3	'20 Seconds To Comply'	13	Timelords
4	Bangles	14	Cyndi Lauper
5	Happy Mondays	15	Phil Collins
6	New Order	16	*1984*
7	Prince	17	Simple Minds
8	Queen	18	Sheena Easton
9	Five Star	19	Duran Duran
10	*The Time*	20	Rolling Stones

B

1	Duran Duran	11	Kool And the Gang
2	Enya	12	Moody Blues
3	Iron Maiden	13	'January'
4	Gene Pitney	14	Mel and Kim
5	Squeeze	15	England World Cup Squad
6	*Beatles For Sale*	16	Deacon Blue
7	Badfinger	17	Smiths
8	*The Rocky Horror Show*	18	Hazel O'Connor
9	'One Night'	19	Adam Faith
10	Sonia	20	Carpenters

C

1	Ten Years After
2	Jesus And Mary Chain
3	Psychedelic Furs
4	Starland Vocal Band
5	1973
6	'A Night At Daddy Gee's'
7	Madness
8	Dan McCafferty
9	Paul Carrack
10	Elbow Bones and the Racketeers
11	Spyro Gyra
12	'Nine a.m., on a New York subway'
13	Cliff Richard
14	Barbara Dickson
15	Bonnie Raitt
16	The Sundays
17	Matt Bianco
18	Ray Davies
19	'Angel Of The Morning'
20	Trinidad Oil Company

24 American Pie

A

1 *Faith*
2 d) 'My Bonnie'
3 His Comets
4 Nancy Sinatra and Frank Sinatra
5 'Ain't No Mountain High Enough'
6 Olivia Newton-John
7 Neil Diamond and Donna Summer
8 'Against All Odds (Take A Look At Me Now)' by Phil Collins
9 'Tammy'
10 'I Want To Hold Your Hand'
11 Peter Cetera
12 'We Are The World'
13 'Red Red Wine' by UB40
14 Stock Aitken Waterman
15 Los Lobos
16 Falco
17 Michael Jackson and Stevie Wonder. The artist named in question C5 would, however, be another clever answer.
18 'Light My Fire'
19 Whitney Houston
20 Elton John, Gladys Knight and Stevie Wonder

B

1 Shaun Cassidy ('Da Doo Ron Ron')
2 'Caribbean Queen (No More Love On The Run)' by Billy Ocean
3 Marilyn Martin
4 c) 'Hound Dog'
5 'Volare'
6 It was titled 'April Love'
7 'Ben'
8 Bobby Vinton
9 'Fingertips – Pt. 2'
10 c) Lorne Greene ('Ringo')
11 Steam
12 '(You're My) Soul And Inspiration'
13 'The Twist' by Chubby Checker
14 George Harrison ('Got My Mind Set On You')
15 Billy Idol
16 Gene Pitney
17 Joe Cocker and Bill Medley
18 Lisa Lisa and Cult Jam
19 *A Summer Place*
20 'Dancing Queen'

C

1 Georgia ('Midnight Train To Georgia', 'Georgia On My Mind' and 'The Night the Lights Went Out in Georgia')
2 a) 'A Big Hunk O'Love'
3 Kyu Sakamoto
4 'Me and Bobby McGee' by Janis Joplin
5 'Uncle Albert/Admiral Halsey'
6 Mothers Fathers Sisters Brothers
7 Rick Dees
8 'Dreams'
9 'Funkytown' by Lipps Inc.
10 'Don't You (Forget About Me)' by Simple Minds
11 The Beaters
12 Jim Lowe
13 *S.W.A.T.*
14 'Gonna Fly Now'
15 'Flashdance ... What A Feeling' by Irene Cara and 'Maniac' by Michael Sembello
16 'Whatever Gets You Through the Night'
17 Glasgow
18 Anton Karas ('The Third Man Theme')
19 'A View To A Kill' by Duran Duran
20 Frankie Avalon, Shocking Blue and Bananarama

25 Cross The Track

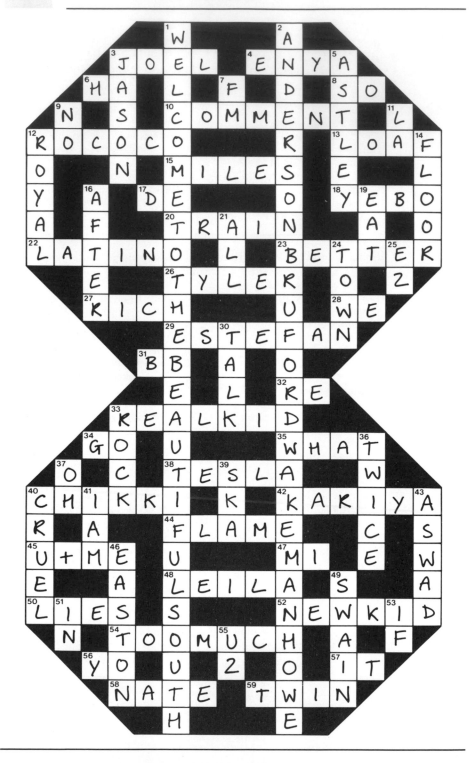

(We Better Go Back)

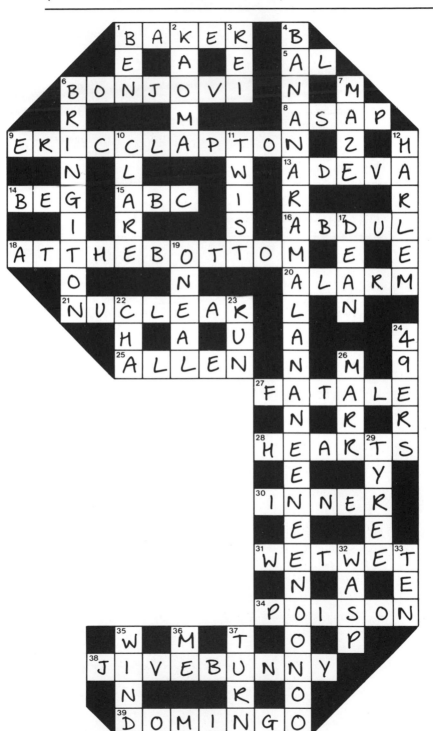

26 Two Out Of Three Ain't Bad

1	Bucks Fizz	11	Donna Summer
2	Cure	12	Eurythmics
3	Diana Ross	13	Kate Bush
4	Aretha Franklin	14	Chris Rea
5	Iron Maiden	15	Simple Minds
6	Gary Numan	16	Elvis Costello
7	Smiths	17	Siouxsie and the Banshees
8	Fleetwood Mac	18	Stranglers
9	Prince	19	Bruce Springsteen
10	UB40	20	Cliff Richard

27 Madchester Rave On

1	Stone Roses	12	Manchester Utd. F.C.
2	808 State	13	Freshies
3	A Guy Called Gerald	14	Simply Red
4	Buzzcocks	15	Elkie Brooks
5	Morrissey	16	Herman's Hermits
6	Hollies	17	10 C.C.
7	Rick Astley	18	Inspiral Carpets
8	Swing Out Sister	19	The Smiths – they all appear
9	Happy Mondays		on single sleeves
10	Joy Division	20	The Fall
11	The Hacienda, and New Order co-owns it		

28 Green Onions

1	UB40	11	Stevie Wonder
2	Odyssey	12	Belinda Carlisle
3	Scritti Politti	13	*Trash*
4	Shakin' Stevens	14	Jam
5	Tom Jones	15	'The Floral Dance'
6	Windsor Davies & Don Estelle	16	Al Green
7	Hollies	17	Heaven 17
8	Move	18	Third World
9	Sting	19	Evelyn Thomas
10	Chris Rea	20	Wurzels

B

1	Jethro Tull	11	Creedence Clearwater Revival
2	Benny Hill	12	Yes
3	Vince Hill (number 2 in 1967)	13	Bryan Ferry
4	Herman's Hermits	14	Michelle Shocked
5	Guns N' Roses	15	Kinks
6	Peter Green	16	Elvis Presley
7	'The Green Manalishi (With A Two Pronged Crown)'	17	Los Lobos
		18	Paul Hardcastle
8	Housemartins	19	X-Ray Spex
9	Boney M	20	Jane Morgan
10	Boomtown Rats		

C

1	Farmers Boys	11	Barry McGuire
2	Kermit The Frog	12	'Gasoline Alley'
3	Buggles	13	John D. Loudermilk
4	Jefferson Airplane	14	Muddy Waters
5	Sammy Hagar	15	Time Zone
6	Heinz	16	A Flux Of Pink Indians
7	*Paint Your Wagon*	17	Jim Lowe, Glen Mason and Frankie Vaughan
8	*Stop The World – I Want To Get Off*	18	That Petrol Emotion
9	Hedgehoppers Anonymous	19	Jimmie Rodgers
10	Jonathan King	20	Benny Green

29 Leave Me Alone

A

Simon & Garfunkel; Kylie Minogue; Simple Minds; Whitney Houston; John Lennon; Julian Cope; Sad Café; Depeche Mode; George Michael; Melle Mel; Kim Wilde; David Bowie; Guns N' Roses; Renee and Renato; Soft Cell. *This leaves* Ono *as the odd one out.*

B

Duran Duran; Luke Goss; Matt Bianco; Band Aid; Bryan Ferry; Michael McDonald; Janet Jackson; Pointer Sisters; Simply Red; Black Box; Deacon Blue; Boy George; Five Star; Then Jerico; London Boys. *This leaves* Plastic *as the odd one out.*

C

Talking Heads; Jive Bunny; Sinead O'Connor; Phil Collins; Cliff Richard; Elton John; Jon & Vangelis; Kelly Marie; Donny Osmond; Spandau Ballet; Rod Stewart; Adam and the Ants; Chas & Dave; Buddy Holly; Don Johnson. *This leaves* Band *as the odd one out.*

By rearranging the three odd words out, you should have found the well known name, *Plastic Ono Band*.

30 Sing Our Own Song

A

1 Caron Wheeler
2 Felly
3 Gary Haisman
4 Adeva
5 Elisa Fiorillo
6 Max Headroom
7 P. P. Arnold
8 Yazz and the Plastic Population
9 Cookie Crew
10 Lisa Stansfield
11 Malcolm McLaren
12 Jellybean
13 Coldcut
14 D. Mob
15 Tyree
16 Beatmasters (and on her own, of course)
17 Blow Monkeys
18 Beats International
19 D. Mob
20 Bomb The Bass

B

1 Gene Pitney
2 Cher
3 Chaka Khan and Ray Charles
4 Sheena Easton
5 Tom Jones
6 Curtis Mayfield
7 Al Green
8 Musical Youth
9 Shirley Bassey
10 Smokey Robinson
11 'Fairytale Of New York'
12 'I Got You Babe' and 'Breakfast In Bed'
13 'In A Lifetime'
14 'Don't Leave Me This Way'
15 'Peter Gunn'
16 'My Love'
17 'The Twist, Yo Twist'
18 'When Love Comes To Town'
19 'Easy Lover'
20 'Come Outside'

C

1 Courtney Pine
2 Billy Preston
3 Hank Marvin
4 Sting
5 Grandmaster Melle Mel
6 Kate Bush
7 Technotronic and Tek 3
8 Heaven 17 and Paul Hardcastle
9 Bomb The Bass and Beatmasters
10 Cocteau Twins
11 Full Force
12 Beach Boys
13 Gary Numan
14 Siedah Garrett
15 Bobby Womack
16 Both featured on hits by Soul II Soul
17 Both featured on hits by the Crusaders
18 Both featured on hits by Simon Harris
19 Living In A Box
20 Eric and the Good Good Feeling and Electribe 101

31 Laugh At Me

A

1 Bananarama
2 'The Chicken Song'
3 The Firm
4 'Shaddup You Face'
5 'Ernie (The Fastest Milkman In The West)'
6 Mel and Kim (Smith and Wilde)
7 Barron Knights
8 Cliff Richard, featuring Hank Marvin
9 neil (Nigel Planer)
10 Ken Dodd
11 Des O'Connor
12 Keith Harris, 'Orville's Song'
13 Rolf Harris
14 Lonnie Donegan
15 Scaffold
16 Paul McCartney
17 'The Laughing Gnome'
18 Billy Connolly
19 Chas & Dave
20 Harry Enfield

B

1 Goodies
2 Rory Bremner
3 Fred Wedlock
4 Jasper Carrott
5 Bernard Cribbins
6 Kenny Everett
7 Black
8 'Happy Talk' by Captain Sensible
9 'Grandad'
10 Roland Rat Superstar
11 Morris Minor and the Majors
12 'Are You Lonesome Tonight'
13 Billie Davis
14 'Whispering Grass' by Windsor Davies & Don Estelle
15 Russ Abbot
16 Black Lace
17 Goons
18 Ray Stevens
19 René and Yvette (Gorden Kaye & Vicki Michelle)
20 Chipmunks

C

1 Max Boyce
2 Dave Lee Travis and Paul Burnett
3 Paul Burnett was the Pee Bee Squad
4 Tommy Cooper
5 Jimmy Tarbuck
6 Jonathan King
7 Charlie Drake
8 'The Army Game'
9 Bernard Bresslaw
10 'Speedy Gonzales'
11 Muppets
12 Roger Kitter
13 Wurzels
14 'You're The One That I Want'
15 'The Trail Of The Lonesome Pine'
16 John Gorman, Chris Tarrant, Sally James and Bob Carolgees
17 John Craven, Noel Edmonds, Keith Chegwin and Maggie Philbin
18 'Snoopy vs. The Red Baron'
19 Napoleon XIV
20 'Smoke Gets In Your Eyes'

32 Year Of Decision

A

1 1989
2 1984
3 1983
4 1987
5 1986
6 1981
7 1988
8 1980
9 1985
10 1982

B

1	1974	6	1978
2	1973	7	1975
3	1971	8	1979
4	1976	9	1977
5	1972	10	1970

C

1	1965	6	1961
2	1969	7	1963
3	1962	8	1966
4	1967	9	1968
5	1964	10	1960

33 Panic

A	Rocket
B	Enya
C	Empty
D	Lillo
E	Ask
F	Roland
G	Off The
H	USA
I	Need You
J	De Do Do Do
K	Tutti
L	Ha Ha
M	EMI
N	Follow Him
O	Otto
P	Up The
Q	No Time To
R	Thin
S	Andy
T	International
U	New
V	Willow
W	Tutu
X	Willies
Y	Swim
Z	Hue
AA	A fee

The quoted song is 'Reel Around the Fountain' by the Smiths. The quote is: "It's time the tale were told / of how you took a child / and you made him old / Reel around the fountain / slap me on the patio / I'll take it now / Fifteen minutes with you / well, I wouldn't say no . . ."
Words by Morrissey, Copyright Control.

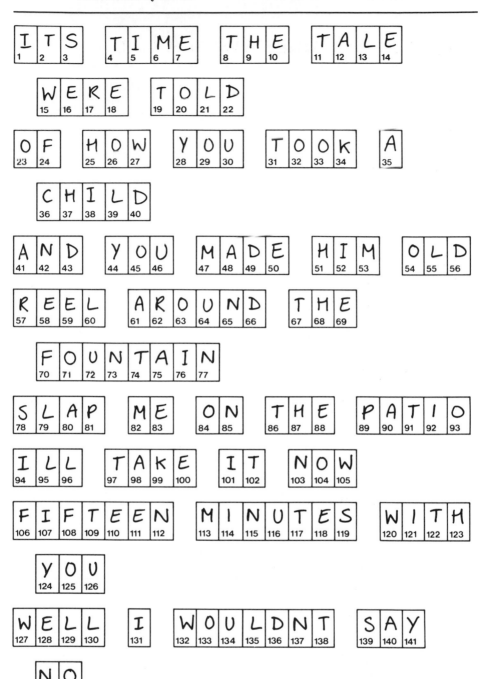

ITS TIME THE TALE

WERE TOLD

OF HOW YOU TOOK A

CHILD

AND YOU MADE HIM OLD

REEL AROUND THE

FOUNTAIN

SLAP ME ON THE PATIO

ILL TAKE IT NOW

FIFTEEN MINUTES WITH

YOU

WELL I WOULDNT SAY

NO

34 Little Things Mean A Lot

A

1 Erasure	11 Litte Richard
2 Police	12 Fleetwood Mac
3 Prince	13 D. Mob
4 Childline charity	14 'A Little More Love'
5 Nicole	15 Little Eva
6 Aneka	16 Rolling Stones
7 Wings	17 Sting
8 'Wake Up Little Susie'	18 Stranglers
9 Dusty Springfield	19 Stevie Nicks
10 Bobby Brown	20 *Popped In Souled Out*

B

1 Bing Crosby	11 Craig Douglas
2 Howard Jones	12 Rick Nelson
3 Bob Marley	13 'Little Sister'
4 Shakin' Stevens	14 Tymes
5 Cliff Richard	15 Tommy Steele
6 Beverley Sisters	16 Sam Brown
7 'You Little Thief'	17 Del Shannon
8 'Crazy Little Thing Called	18 Sweet
Love'	19 Marianne Faithfull
9 Bay City Rollers	20 Showaddywaddy
10 Monkees	

C

1 Shakin' Stevens	12 Little Feat
2 Maureen	13 Dave Berry
3 Leapy Lee	14 Don Henley
4 1964	15 Little Anthony & the
5 Total Contrast	Imperials
6 b) UK	16 'Go Away Little Girl'
7 Johnny Burnette	17 a) Wayne Fontana & the
8 Kursaal Flyers	Mindmenders
9 Talking Heads	18 Little River Band
10 Marty Wilde	19 Elton John
11 Linda Scott	20 Paul Evans

35 The Big One

A

1 Big Country	12 Rolling Stones
2 Big Bopper	13 We've Got A Fuzzbox And
3 Peter Gabriel	We're Gonna Use It
4 Big Fun	14 'Big Bad John'
5 Alphaville	15 'Big Fun'
6 Big Audio Dynamite	16 *The Hounds Of Love*
7 Duran Duran	17 *Make It Big*
8 Elvis Presley	18 'Big Mouth Strikes Again'
9 'Big Girls Don't Cry'	19 'John Wayne Is Big Leggy'
10 Fleetwood Mac	20 They Might Be Giants
11 *Songs From The Big Chair*	

B

1	Kajagoogoo	11	Joni Mitchell
2	Robert Plant	12	'Act Naturally'
3	Barry Biggs	13	Creedence Clearwater Revival
4	Stranglers	14	Fats Domino
5	Sparks	15	*The Big Area*
6	Big Daddy	16	The Big Three
7	Judge Dread	17	The Big Three (again!)
8	Ivor Biggun	18	'Big Ship'
9	Bob Dylan & the Band	19	Four Preps
10	'Groovin'	20	Shirley Bassey

C

1	The Big Sound	10	Big Bam Boo
2	Big Ben Banjo Band	11	Big Daddy Kane
3	Big Brother and the Holding Company	12	Big Sound Authority
4	'Big Decision'	13	Big Supreme
5	Pigbag	14	Elvis Presley
6	Walter Murphy and the Big Apple Band	15	'The Big Hurt'
7	'Mr. Big Stuff'	16	Mr. Big
8	Big Roll Band	17	Billy Joel
9	'Big Time Operator'	18	Four Seasons
		19	Big Dish
		20	Bolshoi

36 I'd Rather Jack

1 Mike Stock, Matt Aitken and Peter Waterman
2 14–18
3 'Goodbye-ee'
4 'The Upstroke'
5 'I'm So Beautiful' by Divine
6 'You Spin Me Round (Like A Record)' by Dead Or Alive
7 Pete Waterman Label
8 'Never Gonna Give You Up' by Rick Astley
9 'Especially For You' by Kylie Minogue and Jason Donovan
10 Because M/A/R/R/S had blatantly sampled SAW's 'Roadblock' without prior permission
11 Scott Robinson
12 Kylie's was 'Tears On My Pillow' by Little Anthony & the Imperials, and Jason's was 'Sealed With A Kiss' by Brian Hyland
13 *Mandy* by Mandy Smith
14 'It's No Secret'
15 'Let It Be' by Ferry Aid, 'Ferry 'Cross The Mersey' by Christians, Holly Johnson, Paul McCartney, Gerry Marsden and Stock Aitken Waterman, 'Do They Know It's Christmas' by Band Aid II
16 Jakie Quartz
17 Sonia Evans
18 Princess and Mel and Kim
19 'Love In The First Degree' by Bananarama
20 Cliff Richard and Donna Summer
21 Pat Sharpe and Mick Brown
22 *Help A London Child*
23 'The Harder I Try' and 'He Ain't No Competition'
24 Big Fun
25 'I Just Don't Have The Heart' (Cliff Richard), 'Take Me To Your Heart' (Rick Astley), 'Hand On Your Heart' (Kylie Minogue), 'Too Many Broken Hearts' (Jason Donovan), 'Listen To Your Heart' (Sonia), 'Love's About To Change My Heart' (Donna Summer), 'My Heart Goes Bang' (Dead Or Alive), 'Cross My Broken Heart' (Sinitta)

37 Starman

A

1 *Dark Side Of The Moon*
2 'Space Oddity'
3 'Ashes To Ashes'
4 'Eve Of The War'
5 *War Of The Worlds*
6 Sigue Sigue Sputnik
7 'Venus'
8 'A Spaceman Came Travelling'
9 Tornados
10 RAH Band
11 Mars
12 *Venus And Mars*
13 'Walking On The Moon'
14 Freddie Mercury
15 The Firm
16 Duran Duran
17 Timelords
18 Curiosity Killed The Cat
19 'Rocket Man'
20 'Life On Mars'

B

1 'Calling Occupants Of Interplanetary Craft'
2 Rick Wakeman
3 Space
4 Pluto Shervington
5 Hooters
6 'Major Tom (Coming Home)'
7 Mud
8 Jellybean
9 Thomas Dolby
10 John Williams
11 'Jupiter'
12 Bonzo Dog Doo Dah Band
13 'Apollo 9'
14 Shocking Blue
15 A Flock Of Seagulls
16 'Star Wars Theme' – Cantina Band
17 'Something's Gotten Hold Of My Heart' by Marc Almond with Gene Pitney
18 Elvis Presley
19 Edie Brickell & the New Bohemians
20 Sarah Brightman

C

1 *Cosmic Thing*
2 'Venus'
3 'Venus In Blue Jeans'
4 Spotnicks
5 Video Kids
6 Space Monkey
7 'Destination Venus'
8 Don Partridge
9 'Space Station No. 5'
10 Slick
11 'Planet Rock'
12 'Purple People Eater'
13 'How High The Moon'
14 'Dynamite'
15 Billy Preston
16 *The Cosmos*
17 Tony Crombie
18 Derrick Morgan
19 Shadows
20 John Denver

38 Si Si Je Suis Un Rock Star

A

1 Los Lobos
2 Spanish
3 'Comment Te Dire Adieu'
4 Kaoma
5 'Begin The Beguine'
6 Julio Iglesias
7 'Joe Le Taxi'
8 'Sukiyaki'
9 Jane Birkin & Serge Gainsbourg
10 Desireless
11 'Moulin Rouge'
12 Kraftwerk
13 Spanish
14 Hebrew
15 Ofra Haza
16 Beatles
17 Sylvia
18 'You Don't Have To Say You Love Me'
19 'La Vie En Rose'
20 German

B

1 Sarah Brightman and Paul Miles-Kingston
2 Steeleye Span
3 'Nunc Dimittis'
4 Zaire
5 'Dominique'
6 Françoise Hardy
7 'Ca Plane Pour Moi'
8 'Chanson D'Amour'
9 Engelbert Humperdinck ('The Last Waltz')
10 Edith Piaf
11 'Volare'
12 'Et Les Oiseaux Chantaient'
13 *A Day At The Races*
14 'GI Blues'
15 'Unhalfbricking'
16 'Rubber Soul'
17 '2001 – A Space Odyssey'
18 German
19 'Mah Na Mah Na'
20 'Dolce Vita'

C

1 Chinese (Mandarin)
2 'Guantanamera' by the Sandpipers
3 Jonathan King
4 'Hare Krishna Mantra'
5 'Ye Ke Ye Ke'
6 'Mamy Blue'
7 'Mustafa' or 'Mustapha'
8 'Il Est Ne Le Divin Enfant'
9 'El Bimbo'
10 Georghe Zamfir
11 Cerrone
12 Monty Sunshine
13 'Diggi Loo-Diggi Ley'
14 Les Compagnons de la Chanson
15 Marino Marini
16 France
17 Severine
18 '99 Luftballons'
19 'Non Ho L'Eta Per Amarti'
20 Japanese

39 Michael Jackson Medley

A

1 'I Just Can't Stop Loving You'
2 'Billie Jean'
3 'The Girl Is Mine'
4 'One Day In Your Life'
5 'Ben'
6 'Bad'
7 'Thriller'
8 'Beat It'
9 'Dirty Diana'
10 'Rockin' Robin'

B

1 'Don't Stop Till You Get Enough'
2 'She's Out Of My Life'
3 'Ain't No Sunshine'
4 'Farewell My Summer Love'
5 'I Want You Back'
6 'ABC'
7 'Show You The Way To Go'
8 'Rock With You'
9 'Blame It On The Boogie'
10 'Can You Feel It'

C

1 'Off The Wall'
2 'Got To Be There'
3 'The Way You Make Me Feel'
4 'I'll Be There'
5 'The Love You Save'
6 'Leave Me Alone'
7 'Wanna Be Startin' Something'
8 'Smooth Criminal'
9 'Say Say Say'
10 'Shake Your Body (Down To The Ground)'

40 Nice Legs Shame About The Face

1 Kid Creole
2 Paula Abdul
3 Paul Young
4 Cher
5 Tina Turner
6 Fat Boys
7 Rod Stewart
8 Queen
9 Gloria Estefan
10 Sheena Easton

1

2

5

6

7

8

9 10

41 Song Sung Blue

A

1	Erasure	12	Glenn Frey
2	Blondie	13	Cliff Richard
3	New Order or Fats Domino	14	Altered Images
4	Neil Diamond	15	Frank Ifield
5	Elton John	16	Justin Hayward and John
6	David Bowie		Lodge
7	Ultravox	17	Roy Orbison
8	Alma Cogan	18	Roy Orbison or Linda
9	Mike Oldfield		Ronstadt
10	ABC	19	Mike Post
11	Paul Quinn and Edwyn Collins	20	Bob Dylan

B

1	Madonna	12	Moody Blues
2	Elvis Costello	13	Blue Mercedes
3	Sting	14	Blue Nile
4	Diana Ross	15	Georgie Fame and the Blue
5	Elvis Presley		Flames
6	Cocteau Twins	16	Blue Oyster Cult
7	Jennifer Warnes	17	Johnny Duncan and the
8	Jesus And Mary Chain		Bluegrass Boys
9	Martin Stephenson and the	18	Blue Mink
	Daintees	19	Bluebells
10	Style Council	20	Blue Zoo
11	Deacon Blue		

C

1 Blue Rondo à la Turk
2 Blue Note
3 Rodgers and Hart
4 Fleetwoods
5 Joliet Jake and Elwood Blues
6 Barry Green
7 David Bowie in 'Sound And Vision'
8 Blue Zone
9 Chelsea, Brighton and Coventry City
10 J. Geils Band
11 'Volare'
12 'Raining In My Heart'
13 'Blue Guitar', which was not an Elvis Presley hit
14 'Blue Christmas', which did not reach number one
15 Michael Jackson

42 Food For Thought

A

1. 'Do They Know It's Christmas'
2. Bananarama
3. Neneh Cherry
4. 'Hot Dog'
5. 'There's A Guy Works Down The Chipshop Swears He's Elvis'
6. Hot Chocolate
7. Coldcut
8. Jam
9. Meatloaf
10. Salt 'n' Pepa
11. 'Sugar Sugar'
12. 'Honey'
13. Jellybean
14. UB40
15. Prefab Sprout
16. Deacon Blue
17. Jasper Carrott
18. 'I Eat Cannibals'
19. Galaxy
20. Bucks Fizz

B

1. Newbeats
2. Searchers
3. Peter Sellers and Sophia Loren
4. Splodgenessabounds
5. 'Yummy Yummy Yummy'
6. Little Richard
7. Russ Conway
8. Donna Summer
9. Wierd Al Yankovic
10. 'Ob-La-Di Ob-La-Da'
11. 'Banana Boat Song'
12. Chrissie Hynde
13. 'Sukiyaki'
14. Brown Sauce
15. Blondie
16. Rolling Stones
17. 'Breakfast In America'
18. Jam
19. Orange Juice
20. Oran 'Juice' Jones

C

1. Slim Dusty
2. The Mince Pies
3. George Clinton
4. Heinz
5. Lemon Pipers
6. Mighty Lemon Drops
7. Street Band
8. Hank Williams
9. ZZ Top
10. 'Popcorn'
11. Blancmange – 'The Day Before You Came'
12. Nancy Whiskey
13. Shadows
14. Suzanne Vega
15. 'You Keep Me Hangin' On'
16. 'Simon Says'
17. 'You Sexy Sugar Plum (But I Like It)'
18. They were all, successively, the Peaches half of the duo Peaches and Herb
19. Electric Prunes
20. Jona Lewie

43 The Letter

A

1 'Hen Will I Be Famous'
2 'Ticket To Rid'
3 'Lad'
4 'Bass In Pocket'
5 'Big Yellow Tax'
6 'Tars On My Pillow'
7 '999'
8 'Stairway To Haven'
9 'Love Sack'
10 'Maggie Ma'
11 'All Me'
12 'The Ower'
13 'Old'
14 'Teddy Bar'
15 'Rock Around The Cock'
16 'He Ain't Heavy, He's My Bother'
17 'Carless Whisper'
18 'It's My Part'
19 'Sand By Me'
20 'Tinted Love'

B

1 'What's Another Ear'
2 'The Greatest Love Of Al'
3 'Godfinger'
4 'Fist Time'
5 'With A Little Help From My Fiends'
6 'Dinner Wit Gershwin'
7 'Your Son'
8 'Con Everybody'
9 'You Can Hurry Love'
10 'What A Wonderful Word'
11 'Man Woman Blues'
12 'Hose Of Fun'
13 'When My Little Girl Is Miling'
14 'Bake Street'
15 'Ban Of Gold'
16 'Pap Don't Preach'
17 'Slop John B.'
18 'Deck Of Cads'
19 'Moments In Sol'
20 'Whiter Shade Of Pal'

C

1 'Get Outta My Reams, Get Into My Car'
2 'Rub Don't Take Your Love To Town'
3 'Get Off Of My Clod'
4 'Evil Woman'
5 'On The Bach'
6 'Upside Dow'
7 'Hat Girl Belongs To Yesterday'
8 'Every Little Thing She Does Is Magi'
9 'Bowing In The Wind'
10 'My Payer'
11 'Chin In Your Hand'
12 'You In Again'
13 'There Ain't Nothing Like Saggin''
14 'Get Read'
15 'Broken Wigs'
16 'Oman In Love'
17 'Red My Lips'
18 'Hat Joke's Not Funny Anymore'
19 'Little Own Flirt'
20 'Don't Lave Me This Way'

44 Calling Your Name

A

1 Hollies
2 Genesis
3 Bucks Fizz
4 UB40
5 Fat Boys
6 Salt 'n' Pepa
7 Blondie
8 Dire Straits
9 From the initials of the four members: (A)gnetha Faltskog, (B)enny Anderson, (B)jorn Ulvaeus and (A)nni Frid Lyngstad
10 From Roxy Music's hit 'Pyjamarama'
11 After two characters in the TinTin cartoons
12 From two of the founding members, Mick *Fleetwood* and John *Mc*Vie
13 They were five brothers with the family name Jackson
14 In *aid* of the Zeebrugge *Ferry* disaster
15 After the lead singer Jon Bon Jovi

B

1 T'Pau
2 Anthrax
3 Frankie Goes To Hollywood
4 All About Eve
5 Jethro Tull
6 B-52s
7 Communards
8 Duran Duran
9 French, 'Hurried Fashion'
10 Latin, 'The Position As It Was'
11 Gaelic, 'Kiss'
12 German, 'Powerplant'
13 Italian (nearly), 'Political Writings'
14 Gaelic, 'Family'
15 Arabic, 'Black'

C

1 Everything But The Girl
2 Eurythmics
3 Bauhaus
4 Icehouse
5 Dexy's Midnight Runners
6 *Clockwork Orange* by Anthony Burgess
7 *Prisoners Of Pain* by Arthur Yanov
8 *The Naked Lunch* by William Burroughs
9 Woody Guthrie's autobiography, *Bound For Glory*
10 *The Hitchhikers Guide To The Galaxy* by Douglas Adams
11 *The Silmarillion* by J. R. R. Tolkien
12 After the ladies kept for the pleasure of the German troops in World War II
13 After the five artists involved: (M)artyn and (S)teve Young, (A)lex, (R)udi and (R)ussell Kane
14 After Georgia bluesmen *Pink* Anderson and *Floyd* Council
15 After two bands the members had previously played with: LA Guns and Hollywood Rose

45 Sunshine On Leith

A

1. 'The Sun Always Shines On TV'
2. David Bowie
3. 'John Kettley (Is A Weatherman)'
4. 'I Wish It Would Rain Down'
5. Status Quo
6. 'The Wind Beneath My Wings'
7. 'It's Raining Men'
8. Bob Dylan
9. Alison Moyet
10. Martika
11. Earth Wind And Fire
12. KC and the Sunshine Band
13. 'It's Raining'
14. 'Hot In The City'
15. Billy Joel
16. Bangles
17. Ritchie Blackmore
18. 'Seasons In The Sun'
19. Four Seasons
20. Kate Bush

B

1. Toyah
2. Buddy Holly
3. Rolf Harris
4. Thunderclap Newman
5. Aswad
6. 'Rainy Night In Georgia'
7. 'Sun City'
8. Lindisfarne
9. Heatwave
10. 'Raindrops Keep Falling On My Head'
11. Walker Brothers
12. Katrina and the Waves
13. 'Sun Street'
14. Rocker's Revenge
15. 'Sunny'
16. Jimi Hendrix
17. 'Purple Haze'
18. Donovan
19. Rainmakers
20. *Raintown*

C

1. 'Whole Lotta Woman'
2. 'The Day The Rains Came'
3. Thomas Dolby
4. Johnny and the Hurricanes
5. 'Wild Wind'
6. 'Wayward Wind'
7. They Might Be Giants
8. 'Farewell My Summer Love'
9. Association
10. 'Rain'
11. 'The Freeze'
12. Kiss
13. Thin Lizzy
14. 'Storms In Africa (Part II)'
15. Three Dog Night
16. Andy Fairweather-Low
17. Dickie Valentine
18. *Bonnie And Clyde*
19. Snow
20. 'Misty'

46 All Those Years Ago

A

1	Housemartins	13	Smiths
2	Bangles	14	Jesus And Mary Chain
3	Madonna	15	Pet Shop Boys
4	Erasure	16	Farley 'Jackmaster' Funk
5	Patti La Belle and Michael McDonald	17	Howard Jones
		18	Furniture
6	Whitney Houston	19	P.I.L.
7	Human League	20	Elkie Brooks
8	Peter Gabriel	21	New Order
9	Paul Simon	22	Suzanne Vega
10	Pete Wylie	23	Gwen Guthrie
11	Art Of Noise featuring Duane Eddy	24	Kate Bush
		25	Bruce Hornsby and the Range
12	David Bowie		

B

1	Sting	14	Cocteau Twins
2	Big Supreme	15	Luther Vandross
3	Everything But The Girl	16	Aretha Franklin
4	Ruby Turner	17	Housemartins
5	We've Got A Fuzzbox And We're Gonna Use It	18	Talk Talk
		19	INXS
6	Smiths	20	Depeche Mode
7	Peter Gabriel	21	Rolling Stones
8	Eurythmics	22	Genesis
9	Anita Baker	23	King Kurt
10	Janet Jackson	24	Bon Jovi
11	Pet Shop Boys	25	Madonna
12	The The		
13	Prince		

C

1	'So Macho/Cruising' by Sinitta	10	Pam and Audrey Hall
2	*Graceland* by Paul Simon	11	*Hunting High And Low* by A-Ha
3	They all had hits thanks to Levi Jeans commercials	12	Norway (A-Ha), Sweden (Europe), Ireland (Chris De Burgh), Jamaica (Boris Gardiner) and Austria (Falco)
4	*True Blue* by Madonna, *The Seer* by Big Country and *Revenge* by Eurythmics	13	'That's What Friends Are For' by Dionne Warwick and Friends
5	The Bee Gees		
6	Roxy Music/Bryan Ferry and Police	14	Anita Dobson, Nick Berry, Letitia Dean and Paul Medford
7	'Living Doll' and 'Spirit In The Sky'	15	Berlin
8	Frank Sinatra		
9	Erasure		

47 Word Up

A

1. ROXY MUSIC
2. RICK ASTLEY
3. MADNESS
4. UNDERTONES
5. GARY NUMAN
6. ELTON JOHN
7. PAULA ABDUL

B

1. CAT STEVENS
2. ELAINE PAIGE
3. WHITNEY HOUSTON
4. RANDY CRAWFORD
5. FIVE STAR
6. MARVIN GAYE
7. SLADE
8. RINGO STARR

C

1. KATE BUSH
2. BING CROSBY
3. KYLIE MINOGUE
4. WHO
5. MATT BIANCO
6. MARILLION
7. BAD MANNERS
8. DIRE STRAITS

48 American Trilogy

A

1	New York City	11	Las Vegas
2	San Jose	12	Memphis
3	Chicago	13	Seattle
4	Harlem	14	Philadelphia
5	L.A.	15	Milwaukee
6	Miami	16	Kansas City
7	New Orleans	17	Manhattan
8	New York	18	Detroit City
9	Anchorage	19	Nashville
10	San Francisco	20	New York and L.A.

B

1	Illinois	11	Arkansas
2	New Jersey	12	Georgia
3	Hawaii	13	Indiana
4	New York	14	Michigan
5	Utah	15	Texas
6	Ohio	16	Massachusetts
7	North Dakota	17	Alabama
8	Mississippi	18	Pennsylvania
9	Minnesota	19	Virginia
10	Tennessee	20	California

C

1	Beatles	11	Herman's Hermits
2	Barry Manilow	12	Sly and the Family Stone
3	Bay City Rollers	13	Lulu
4	Stevie Wonder	14	Andy Gibb
5	Neil Sedaka	15	Olivia Newton-John
6	Cher	16	Huey Lewis and the News
7	John Denver	17	Earth Wind And Fire
8	Daryl Hall and John Oates	18	Eagles
9	Donny Osmond	19	Bee Gees
10	Dawn	20	Simon and Garfunkel

49 I'm Just A Singer (In A Rock 'N' Roll Band)

A

1	Wet Wet Wet	13	A-Ha
2	Bon Jovi	14	Simple Minds
3	U2	15	Dead or Alive
4	Pet Shop Boys	16	Climie Fisher
5	T'Pau	17	INXS
6	Bros	18	Human League
7	Duran Duran (or Arcadia)	19	Fine Young Cannibals
		20	Transvision Vamp
8	Pretenders	21	Then Jerico
9	Erasure	22	Spandau Ballet
10	Imagination	23	Madness
11	Level 42	24	Bad Manners
12	Simply Red	25	Curiosity Killed The Cat

B

1	Annie Lennox	13	Ian Astbury
2	Martin Fry	14	Shane McGowan
3	W. Axl Rose	15	Ricky Ross
4	Levi Stubbs	16	Richard Darbyshire
5	Barney Sumner (Bernard Albrecht)	17	Roddy Frame
		18	Eddi Reader
6	Larry Blackmon	19	John Lydon
7	Paul Weller	20	Robert Smith
8	Lemmy	21	Wayne Hussey
9	Paul Heaton	22	Stuart Adamson
10	Dave Gahan	23	Bruce Dickinson
11	Brinsley Forde	24	Noddy Holder
12	Martin Degville	25	Green Gartside

C

1	Matt Bianco	14	Alarm
2	Everything But The Girl	15	Darts
3	Yello	16	XTC
4	Breathe	17	Rush
5	Aerosmith	18	Nena
6	Stone Roses	19	Wonder Stuff
7	Icehouse	20	Europe
8	Texas	21	China Crisis
9	Foreigner	22	Herman's Hermits
10	And Why Not	23	Go West
11	Poison	24	Swing Out Sister
12	Waterboys	25	Stray Cats
13	Killing Joke		

50 The Final Countdown

1 The Lotus Eaters (no. 15 in 1983)
2 Natalie Cole (no. 2 in 1989)
3 Fred Wedlock (no. 6 in 1981)
4 Sex Pistols (no. 6 in 1979)
5 Bellamy Brothers (no. 3 in 1979)
6 Tom Jones (no. 8 in 1967) (Bobby Bare had the original US hit in 1963)
7 Dire Straits (no. 16 in 1985, but it was also a no. 1 album)
8 Chuck Berry (no. 3 in 1964)
9 Madonna (no. 5 in 1985)
10 Bruce Springsteen (no. 16 in 1984)
11 Paul McCartney (no. 32 in 1990)
12 Paul McCartney & Wings (no. 3 in 1974)
13 Beatles (no. 1 in 1968)
14 Re-Flex (no. 28 in 1984)
15 Carly Simon (no. 10 in 1987)
16 George Michael (no. 13 in 1988)
17 Abba (no. 1 in 1977)
18 E-Zee Posse (no. 15 in 1990)
19 Big Country (no. 17 in 1983)
20 Talking Heads (no. 6 in 1985)
21 Hot Chocolate (no. 7 in 1982)
22 Des O'Connor (no. 4 in 1968)
23 Culture Club (no. 3 in 1982)
24 Don McLean (no. 2 in 1972)
25 Maceo & the Macs (no. 54 in 1987)
26 Meatloaf (no. 32 in 1978)
27 Happy Mondays (no. 19 in 1989)
28 Booker T and the MGs (no. 7 in 1980)
29 Michael Jackson (no. 2 in 1989)
30 UB40 (no. 5 in 1986)
31 Sonny (no. 9 in 1965)
32 Three Degrees (no. 13 in 1974)
33 Smiths (no. 11 in 1986)
34 Kitty Kallen (no. 1 in 1954) (Alma Cogan also hit the charts with this song)
35 Black (no. 54 in 1988)
36 The Reynolds Girls (no. 8 in 1989)
37 David Bowie (no. 10 in 1972)
38 Bill Wyman (no. 14 in 1981)
39 Ashaye (no. 45 in 1983)
40 Monks (no. 19 in 1979)
41 Neil Diamond (no. 14 in 1972)
42 UB40 (no. 4 in 1980) (The Barron Knights had a small hit in 1979 with this title)
43 Box Tops (no. 5 in 1967) (Joe Cocker, Amii Stewart, The Mindbenders and The Long And The Short have also had smaller hits with this title)
44 Marilyn (no. 4 in 1983)
45 The Proclaimers (no. 41 in 1988)
46 George Harrison (no. 13 in 1981)
47 Cameo (no. 3 in 1986)
48 Elvis Presley (no. 8 in 1972) (The original version by Mickey Newbury reached no. 42 in 1972)
49 Moody Blues (no. 36 in 1973)
50 Europe (no. 1 in 1986)